GREAT MINDS

Your World...Your Future...YOUR WORDS

From Essex
Edited by Heather Killingray

 Young**Writers**

First published in Great Britain in 2005 by:
Young Writers
Remus House
Coltsfoot Drive
Peterborough
PE2 9JX
Telephone: 01733 890066
Website: www.youngwriters.co.uk

SB ISBN 1 84460 692 9

Foreword

This year, the Young Writers' 'Great Minds' competition proudly presents a showcase of the best poetic talent selected from over 40,000 up-and-coming writers nationwide.

Young Writers was established in 1991 to promote the reading and writing of poetry within schools and to the youth of today. Our books nurture and inspire confidence in the ability of young writers and provide a snapshot of poems written in schools and at home by budding poets of the future.

The thought, effort, imagination and hard work put into each poem impressed us all and the task of selecting poems was a difficult but nevertheless enjoyable experience.

We hope you are as pleased as we are with the final selection and that you and your family continue to be entertained with *Great Minds From Essex* for many years to come.

Contents

Jade Walker (11)	15
Scott Horsnell (12)	15
Tracey Archer (15)	16
Emma Ali (11)	17
Thomas South (11)	18
Georgia Pike (12)	18
Jasmine Hodgkins (11)	19
Jake Hughes (8)	19
Alix Willmore (11)	20
Rebecca Hampson (11)	20
Sarah Cleland (11)	21
Anna Page (11)	21

Hassenbrook School

Matthew Vear (14)	22
Harry Martin (12)	22
Kathryn Biddle (15)	23
Abbie Hughes (14)	23
Andrea Pollard (13)	24
Emma Richardson (14)	24
Rebecca Knight (12)	25
Jamie Dennis (13)	25
Charlie Martin (12)	26
Bradleigh Catmore (11)	26
Elinor Rew (13)	27
Charlotte Dickinson (14)	28
Amy Willson (11)	28
James Bradley (13)	29
Leeanna Davies (13)	29
Chay Appleyard (14)	30
Danielle Thompson (12)	31
Christopher Taylor-Webb (12)	31
Jade Hales (12)	32
Michael Ellis (13)	32
Elizabeth Ebdale (14)	33
Leya Pullen (12)	33
Charlotte Cape (14)	34
Katharine Robson (13)	34
Natalie Gannon (13)	35
Jake Brindley (12)	35
Megan Potts (13)	36

Leanne Briggs (12)	57
Claire Wilson (12)	57
Grace Sussex (13)	58
Robert Clark (13)	59
Laura Martin (14)	59
Louise Wood (14)	60
Sammy Foot (13)	60
Funmike Meheux (13)	61
Simon Apen-Sadler (13)	61
Bethany Harnwell (12)	62
Elisabeth Mann (13)	63
Scott Tuffey (13)	64
Nathan Bull (12)	64
Sammy Hills (12)	65
Elizabeth Fashanu (11)	65
Ryan Burnett (13)	66
Ella Williams (12)	67
Daniel Ridley (13)	68
Chantelle Carter (13)	68
Jennifer Alderslade (11)	69
Jessica Rix (12)	69
Adam Spilsbury (12)	70
Daniel Haywood (13)	70
Daniella Green (12)	71
Ope Ore (11)	71
Katie Fox (13)	72
Joe Shelden (11)	72
Amy Munro (13)	73
Emma Tucker (13)	73
Evan Burrows (12)	74
Laura Jefferson (12)	74
Ryan Harris (11)	75
Tom Smee (11)	75
Emily Butler (11)	76
Jenna James (14)	77
Shallece Bernard (11)	78
Nicholas Metcalfe (11)	78
Charlotte Watts (13)	79
Rebecca Harris (13)	79
Stephanie Randleson (13)	80
Darryl Wyatt (11)	80
Edward Douglas Melrose (11)	81

Jack Sullivan (11)	81
Michael Chaplin (13)	82
Tom Pockett (13)	82
Rebecca Hawkins (13)	83
Lloyd Anderson (13)	83
Nadene Kennedy (13)	84
Faye McInerney (14)	84
Victoria Coleman (13)	85
Hayley Stubbington (13)	85
Constantinos Panayi (11)	86
Sean Wade (12)	86
Laura Pickess (13)	87
Billy Miller (11)	87
Sarah Bonnici (13)	88
Reece Spencer (12)	88
Adam Oxley (13)	89
Neil Moran (12)	89
Michael Ireland (13)	90
Ian Hayfield (12)	90
Samantha Jenkins (14)	91
Rose Pettit (12)	91
Jessica Saville (13)	92
Terry Bradbrook (13)	92
Nicky Wells (13)	93
Marianna Alexandrou (13)	93
Ashleigh Couchman (11)	94
Gabriel Adedipe (11)	94
Lauren Connelly (11)	95
John Wilson (13)	95
Jamie Keddy (13)	96
Samuel Watson (11)	96
Sebastian Massart (13)	97
Siân Roberts (11)	97
Katie Markham (13)	98
George James Hills (11)	98
Francesca Harper (13)	99
Matthew Peacock (13)	99
Daniel Hooper (13)	100
Catherine Hutchinson (12)	100
Lisa Chong (13)	101
Zac Chouman (13)	101
Scott Jenkins (13)	102

Shenfield High School

The Poems

Midnight Fear

At night I lie in the shaft of light from the curtain,
Heart racing, head spinning.
I laugh at my stupidity, but the laugh is nervous.

Trying not to think of the image
Of the peeling, rotting, disappearing flesh I painted in my mind,
I turn over covering my ears.
You'll be like that one day, I whisper to myself.

I shiver all night, although I'm not cold,
Drifting into dreams so graphic that I wake up crying.
When first light comes, the fear numbs and I get a few hours sleep.

The fear dissolves until the next night when it all floods back to me.
I smile at how silly I am being,
But I still hug my knees to my chest as I sleep.

Clare McDonald (15)
Braeside School

What A Day!

Flip, flop
Get the map
Brother's at the top
Mum's gone pop
Dad's a cop
This has got to stop.

Cat's gone stray,
Bills to pay,
Grandma's run away
My auntie eats hay
My sister wants to play
What a day!

Harriet Peachey (13)
Braeside School

My Dog Lucy

It can't be true
I won't believe
It's so overwhelming
I can't breathe.

A light goes on
In my head
'She's going to die,'
The voice in my mind said.

My lovely dog Lucy
She's made me proud
But now it's time
For her last bow.

'It's time to go
To the vet,' Mum said.
'It's time for Lucy to sleep
Forever in her bed.'

She made me laugh
She made me cry
But now it's time
To say goodbye!

Hayley Docker (14)
Braeside School

Going Adrift

I'm moving soon,
I'm going away,
No matter how much I beg to stay,
I asked them why we had to go,
It was hard for them to say,
So why is it when I make some friends,
We always seem to slip away?

Daisy Rankin (13)
Braeside School

Dogs

Some dogs drool, some dogs crawl,
Some try to talk, some like to walk.
Some dogs hate cats, all cats hate rats.
Some have long hair, and some don't care.
Some dogs love food, some get in bad moods,
I love them they're so cute; it's a shame they're so mute.

Michelle Taylor (13)
Braeside School

The Black Rose

A black rose as dark as night,
The leaves seem green and bright.
It lies on the ground,
Asleep with no sound.

The thorns are sharp like daggers,
I pick it up and it draws blood.

Jessica Woolf (13)
Braeside School

Squashed In Tightly

The feeling of not being able to breathe
Is when you're squashed in tightly
The sweeping dizzy feelings
Is when you're squashed in tightly
The feeling of when you're tight-chested
Is when you're squashed in tightly
The feeling of being hot and panicked
Is when you're squashed in tightly
The feeling that all your oxygen has left you
Is when you're squashed in tightly.

Sophie Heatley (14)
Braeside School

Leaving Today

My dogs had to leave
On a weekend day,
The big man came
And took them away.

I asked my mum,
'Why is that man
Taking the dogs
In that big red van?'

She looked at me
And then she cried,
I looked at her,
She could not lie.

'The dogs are going
To a nicer place,
Where they can run
And win a race.'

I ran upstairs,
And thought awhile.
I looked at pictures
To make me smile.

I look back now,
At that day,
And then sit down
And start to pray.

I hope that my dogs
Are both alright,
And I hope they know
I think of them every night.

Leanne Frost (14)
Braeside School

Follow Your Dreams

Follow your dreams,
Wherever they lead,
Don't be distracted by
Less worthy needs.

Shelter them, nourish them,
Help them to grow,
Let your heart hold them
Down deep where dreams go.

Be faithful, be loyal,
Then all your life through,
The dreams that you follow
Will keep coming true.

Katerina Pastou (14)
Braeside School

Parachute Jump

Jumping out
Falling down
Whooshing past
Falling fast.

Seeing nothing
Blurring past
Yelling loud
Shouting proud.

Parachute up
Floating down
Seeing target
Thumping down.

Zoe Charge (13)
Braeside School

Rabbits' Day Out

Rabbits small, rabbits tall,
Bounce, bounce, bounce.
Through the green, green grass.
Bounce, bounce, bounce.
Jumping, leaping through the farmer's land.
Bounce, bounce, bounce, *bang!*

Nicola Lambrianos (14)
Braeside School

Bubbles

Blow. blow
Blow bubbles
Blow, blow
Blow bubbles
Thin and transparent
Flying in the air
In a world of their own, never with a home
Blow, blow
Pop!

Minnie Johal (13)
Braeside School

White Dream

Winter sweeps over us,
Trailing her white silk cloak behind,
Leaving the world in a white dream.

Natalie Stone (12)
Braeside School

Summer Sunrise

The warm summer night horizon,
Staring straight at me,
Watching the slow movements I make,
The wind swiftly swaying,
The bright oranges, the glazing blacks,
The shiny yellows, the pearly pinks,
Gives me the warning, sunrise is coming here!

Danielle Conway (12)
Braeside School

Ice Cream

Ice cream cones in different flavours
Flakes, sprinkles and even wafers.
Chocolate, strawberry and vanilla too
Try them all to see which suits you!

Ciara Patel (13)
Braeside School

Nonsense Cat Scratching

The cat's smiling greedy eyes,
Rabbit's grooming cautiously
'Phfit phfit ne ne,'
Fat tummy flopping bromtiously.

Stomp, shromp, clomp, chomp
Big bang theory
'Phfit phfit,' goes the cat
Its whiskers cheery.

Bhavini Gohil (13)
Braeside School

Tear From The Eye

I'm all alone deep and hollow
All I see is pain and sorrow
I have no one to dry my tears
I have no one to wash away my fears.

Rocio Collins (13)
Braeside School

Moon

A giant spotlight.
A big shining moon of cheese,
High up in the sky.

Chloe O'Connor (11)
Braeside School

Always Watching Me

It's always watching me,
That spooky thing.
It's got branches like veins,
That spread all around.
It's always watching me,
Swaying in the breeze.

Tamzin Shepherd (12)
Braeside School

The Giant

Like an octopus with a thousand arms
It makes me feel small
But not as small as the deep purple coloured flowers.

Jessica-Maria Rivas Furlong (12)
Braeside School

Tree In The Sky

Thick and swaying with grace,
Like a creature with millions of arms
Teaching its classroom of ants.

Francesca Higgins (12)
Braeside School

An Autumn Horse-Chestnut Tree

The hazelnut conkers zip up their spiky jackets,
Ready for the fall.

The dehydrated leaves,
Swirl softly to the floor.

The children in the parks,
Play in the leaves.

Waiting 'til they have to stand up tall,
Waiting for the leaves to fall.

Alexandra Jack (12)
Braeside School

The Coal Fire

Like black cocoa-dusted truffles
Dying in the heat, slowly crumbling
Then suddenly saved by a turn of a hand.

Zeinab Harding (12)
Braeside School

Spring Flowers In The Breeze - Haiku

Dainty petals sway
As the bells are ringing out
Soundlessly they call.

Isabelle Docker (12)
Braeside School

Why Am I So Small?

The tree stands so tall, so why am I small?
Me, the flower, so meek and gentle, the tree so big and heavy
He is the Empire State Building and I am the small child below.

Jenna Brown (12)
Braeside School

Pearly White Flowers

Pearly white flowers dangling close to the ground.
Gently swaying there not making a sound.
Like little faces all soft and round.

Skye Jacobs (12)
Braeside School

A Monster Of A Man

A gigantic man as tall as tall can be
His thousands of arms spread out like open fans.
With a village of shivering people looking up at him.

Lucy Brunt (12)
Braeside School

Tree Beyond The Clouds

Climbing to the top,
On an everlasting ladder
Going to catch a cloud.

Rebecca Bushell (12)
Braeside School

Summer Is Here

She walks along the sandy shore.
Her beautiful blue eyes gleam like diamonds.
The wind whips through her long blonde hair,
Summer is here.

Abby Calderwood (12)
Braeside School

Spring Playing

Spring is like a young girl, playing with a ball
Flowers are dancing as they open
A dimmer switch is slowly being turned off as the day ends.

Charlotte Barton (12)
Braeside School

Black Is . . .

Black is death
Black is cold
Black is scary
Black is bold

Black is suffering
Black is pain
Black is night
Will always be the same

Black is space
Black is dark
Black is haunting
Black hides the spark

Black is hiding
Black is black
Black is lonely
Black is back.

Joshua Mower (14)
Clacton County High School

I Love You

I love you
And you love me
I thought it was easy as ABC
You made me upset
You made me hurt
You never tried
I knew it wouldn't work
You didn't think
You didn't see
I really thought it was meant to be

I love you
And you love me
I thought it was easy as ABC
You made me upset
You made me hurt
You never tried
I knew it wouldn't work
You didn't think
You didn't see
You never thought you would lose me.

Katie Hipkin (15)
Clacton County High School

Sport Cars

Sports cars are very fast, they blast
The normal cars off the road.
Sports cars can really blast
Especially with nitrous
Grip tyres can really go
And stop you losing control
Weight reduction kit on the double
Or you'll get in trouble
Turbo go faster
So you'll never find them
Forever.

James Button (12)
Clacton County High School

The Countryside

The countryside is peaceful,
Not a building in sight,
The skies are filling with birds,
Singing whilst taking flight.
The trees are dancing in the wind,
Amongst the forest plants,
Predators hiding in the bushes,
Waiting for their chance.
The fields are stocked with flowers,
Reds, yellows, greens and blues,
A cow stands silently eating,
The grass and leaves he chews.
The sun is rising in the east,
Ready for the dawn,
The woodland creatures all awake,
Deer running with their fawn.
Animals of every kind,
Are at home in the countryside,
No one to disturb them,
On the land - far and wide.
The fresh spring rain starts to fall,
Upon the all-green land,
The rain brings unfamiliar smells,
Of sea water and of sand.
And all the while, everything,
Is in its own certain place,
Plants, trees, bumblebees,
And animals giving chase.
The countryside is peaceful
Not a person in sight,
The skies are clear of birds,
As day has turned to night.

Francesca Rose Sharp (14)
Clacton County High School

Old Friend, New Friend

In Year 4 a new girl came
And Rosie was her name.

I had to show her round the school
I think I showed her every wall.

After that we became best friends
Hopefully friendship never ends.

Now we're in County High
We both have to wear a tie.

We've both made new friends now
But we still keep in touch.

I have made new friends now,
So has she.

I feel like I have a thousand friends now,
There's Louise and Georgia, Alex and Jade, Sasha and Lucy,
And much more.

Alice Pettitt (11)
Clacton County High School

Football

The football match has just started,
Crowds are still pouring in,
The rain has just turned to sunshine,
Everyone is having fun.

Half-time has just begun,
Everyone still having fun
People go and get some food,
And other things too.

End of the match, we score,
Everyone just screaming
'Hip, hip hooray!'

Shai Cutts (12)
Clacton County High School

Old Friend, New Friend

My old friend is Kerry!
Kerry is as pretty as a picture!
Kerry is as chatty as a chatterbox!
Kerry is as wild as a tiger!
Kerry is as loud as a megaphone!
Kerry is as funny as a clown!
Kerry is as giggly as a giggly person!
Kerry is my old friend!

My new friend is Faye!
Faye is as kind as a friend can be!
Faye is as energetic as an athlete!
Faye is as quiet as a mouse!
Faye is as fast as a cheetah!
Faye is as calm as a still pond!
Faye is as good as gold!
Faye is as clever as a stick!
Faye is my new friend!

Jade Walker (11)
Clacton County High School

German Shepherds

German shepherds are nice dogs.
German shepherds chase frogs.
German shepherds eat well.
German shepherds like to pearl.
German shepherds like to dream.
German shepherds like to swim in streams.
German shepherds like to wee.
German shepherds like a lot to see.
German shepherds have black and brown fur.
German shepherds like to chase cats that purr.
German shepherds like the sea.
German shepherds like me.

Scott Horsnell (12)
Clacton County High School

The Imagination

The imagination,
It's a wonderful thing.
You can think, you can be, anyone you want to be.
You can live anywhere, somewhere more exotic.
You can live somewhere, where there is no pain.
Where there is no war, no death, no suffering.

In your imagination,
You can be free,
Be anyone you want to be.
A celebrity, an explorer, an astronaut.
You can live in a happy world, in a happy life.
You can live in a world that you control.

In your imaginary world,
It could be full of sweets, of music, of anything.
You can live in paradise,
Live with the people you want to.
A world without annoying siblings,
Without parents controlling you.
A world like no other.

The imagination,
What an amazing adventure it can hold.
It could hold a romantic journey,
A journey which holds the key to a happy future.

The imagination,
It's wonderful.

Tracey Archer (15)
Clacton County High School

Old Friends, New Friends

When I was five I made a friend, Charlotte, her name was to be,
We danced, we played, we even wore each other's shoes.

When I was six we were still friends,
And staying at each other's houses was our thing to do.

Then I became seven, and so did my friend,
And growing up together was our thing to do,
We enjoyed each other's company
Charlotte knew me inside out, she didn't need a clue.

When we were eight we ventured beyond the gate,
A brave thing for us to do.

Then a few years went by and still our friendship grew,
And then came our biggest change, high school was to come.
We worried together and helped each other.

But all ended well when the first day came and went
I can always rely on Charlotte and she can rely on me,
And after that we both went home together for tea.

The great thing about our friendship
Is that there's always room for others,
And from two grew to four,
And four to six,
And now we have new *friends, friends, friends!*

There should never be a bad ending to friendship
Because friendship never ends!

Emma Ali (11)
Clacton County High School

Old Friend, New Friend

My new friend is called Nathen; he is so fun just like the sun.
Nathen is good at football; he is the best in the west.
Nathen's eyes are as blue as the sky.
When Nathen cooks bangers they go bang in his belly.
Nathen hates his sister, and his sister hates him too.

My old friend is so cool just like a pool.
Sam is so funny just like a clown.
Sam's hair is like spikes,
Sam's hair is black as a cat.
Sam has a smile all the time.
Sam's eyes are blue as the sky.

Thomas South (11)
Clacton County High School

Old Friends And New Friends

You ask me, 'Who is your old friend?'
'My old friend is Jade, when we are together it's like
a never-ending roller coaster.'

You ask me, 'Who is your new friend?'
'April,' I say. 'She has big green eyes and when we
are together, it's like we have had laughing gas,
we never stop.'

You ask me, 'Why do you like them so much?'
'I like them because they are both like me,
we are like bubbles in a bath, popping with laughter.'

You ask me, 'Why are they your best friends?'
I reply with, 'I don't know why, they just are,
it's hard to explain.'

You ask me, 'Will they always be your friends?'
'Yes of course they will be, they are my best friends
and always will be, they are the best friends anyone could have.'

Georgia Pike (12)
Clacton County High School

Old Friends, New Friends

Old friends, new friends
Going to different schools
Maybe never to be seen again.

New friends ready to be made
Laura Gardener, Anna Page
Old friends leaving forever
Emine, Ahmet and Cevher.

Cevher has blue eyes and rather bushy hair
Anna wears glasses but doesn't seem to care.

New school's bigger
Old school's familiar
Old friends fading away
New friends made each day.

More friends waiting in the big wide world
Maybe we'll meet again one day soon.

Jasmine Hodgkins (11)
Clacton County High School

Skateboarding

Sam the silly skater skated to Shaun's house.
Sam and Shaun skated to the skate park.

Sam showed Shaun his Sidewalk Magazine.
Shaun showed Sam his double heel flip.
Shaun saw his friend Scott.

Scott showed them his new skateboard.
Sam, Shaun and Scott skateboarded down to the seaside.

Sam skated down to Woolworths in the town
To buy the song; SK8 Rock.

Sam, Shaun and Scott skated back to their houses
And decided to skate another day.

Jake Hughes (8)
Clacton County High School

Old Friends, New Friends

Shannon was my old friend
She really made me laugh
She was really clever and
Wasn't at all daft.

She was a School Council Member
I wanted to be one too
She was my arch enemy
Now it's all over, *phew!*

Abby is my new friend
She really makes me smile
She really likes me
I've only known her for a while

She is a Form Rep
I wanted to be as well
But I still like her (not) only joking!
She can't tell.

Alix Willmore (11)
Clacton County High School

Old Friend, New Friend

Casey is as small as a baby
She has hair as long as a stick
Casey crunches chicken nuggets
Her best colour is blue
She always gets the flu
Casey says 'Snap Crackle Pop'
Her bell goes ding dong.

Sarah has green eyes like grass
She acts like a clown
Also she likes to wear a gown
Sarah has hair as brown as brass
She always picks up grass
Pitter patter she likes fish on batter
That is why she is my friend.

Rebecca Hampson (11)
Clacton County High School

Old Friend, New Friend

Billie-Rose has long brown hair
When she wakes up in the morning she's as grumpy as a bear
She likes eating curry
When it's hot she eats it in a hurry
She's as skinny as a stick
She says Sims is so cool
She likes buying clothes and shoes at the mall.

Rebecca's favourite sport is tennis
She's as naughty as Dennis the Menace
When she starts to make popcorn the microwave goes . . .
Pop! Ping! Bang!
Rebecca's hair is as orange as orange juice
Rebecca likes licking her lovely lolly
She has a bird called Polly.

Sarah Cleland (11)
Clacton County High School

Old Friend, New Friend

Old school, new school,
Old friends, new friends,
Old friend always there for me,
New friend, nice and kind to me.

They are funny and kind,
And sharing and caring,
Jasmine with blue eyes,
And Laura with brown,
For them it's thumbs up,
And not thumbs down.

Old friends, new friends,
Old school, new school,
Same school, same friends,
Whatever kind of friends they are,
They'll always be my friends.

Anna Page (11)
Clacton County High School

Khronos' Decay

Motionless, sitting in a murky puddle of water and algae,
Covered in a layer of fermenting effluence, symbolising the filth of time.
A stench, of utter distaste, drifting airily around the room,
If one was to enter, one would be compelled to turn.
Due to the bitter remnants of time, and to gaze upon something,
Which had once been a tower of beautiful glory,
Would cause one to think, what evil forces of time can change
A once magnificent item, to a mass of decaying disfigurement?
And then the answer hits you, only time can tell.

Matthew Vear (14)
Hassenbrook School

Me, My Friends

Across the playground I run,
Me, my friends having fun,
Not a care in the world,
Me, my friends having fun.

Across the playground I run,
Me, my friends having fun,
No strains, no pain,
Me, my friends having fun.

Me, my friends,
Always together,
Nothing can split us,
Always together.

Me, my friends,
Always together,
We're as tight as can be,
Me, my friends,
Always together.

Harry Martin (12)
Hassenbrook School

Snowflakes

Sparkling snowflakes, crystal clear,
Some sharp, some gentle, but nothing to fear.

As white as snow, as clear as glass,
Glistening and shining on the covered grass.

Like fields of candyfloss, crispy white,
Falling and drifting from the cold air night.

Every part different, all shapes and sizes,
The starlit sky, continuous white sheets.

Footsteps, a crunching sound,
Snowflakes shimmering, all beauty found.

The sun beaming down, a loss of twinkle,
The melting stage, the shape has broken.

Kathryn Biddle (15)
Hassenbrook School

A Rose

A fiery red petal lying on the ground,
One day it's going to be kept and found.

Romantic, and a soft sweet smell,
Lying at the bottom of a dark, cold well.

A prick of the thorn can make you bleed,
But this little thing does a lot of deed.

It is one thing that people admire,
Memories can explode like a fire.

Love is the meaning of this flower,
A long line of them hanging from a tower.

That thing I'm describing is a rose,
And has a meaning to say, 'I love you loads.'

Abbie Hughes (14)
Hassenbrook School

In Your Dreams

In your dreams, you can fly,
You can soar, through the sky.
In your dreams, you can do anything
That you want to.

In your dreams, you can be a star,
You can go far,
In your dreams, you can achieve anything
That you want to.

In your dreams, you can have anything you wish,
You can be with anyone that you've missed,
In your dreams, you can have anything
That you want to.

In real life you would fall, not fly
In real life you can get hurt and die,
But in your dreams, you can do anything
That you want to.

Andrea Pollard (13)
Hassenbrook School

Roses And Snowflakes

Hearts of the earth
Diamonds of the sky
Blood-like petals
Soft to touch
Sweet to smell
Every one of the glittering crystals
Different
As they fall from Heaven
Like angels
A bundle of love to hold in your
Hands
Like lace blowing in the wind.

Emma Richardson (14)
Hassenbrook School

Tear Of Life

Take a tear of a broken soul
A piece of grass from Mother Nature itself
A piece of hair, black as coal
And also loving good health

A beautiful smile with lips so pink
Small fingers and toes, oh so smooth
Blue shiny eyes, so she can blink
With legs and arms to help her move

Give her a heart and keep it beating
With blood to make her heart pump
And skin to keep her body heating
And shoulders so that she does not slump

Give her a child and a loving man
A ready-made family full of affection and love
Her whole life and family squished in a can
And her guiding angel up from above

Don't take advantage of your life today
Don't be scared of terror
Thank God your heart's beating day after day
You know you won't live forever.

Rebecca Knight (12)
Hassenbrook School

Recipe For A Special Girlfriend

In order to make a special girlfriend,
You will need the following ingredients:
First you must take a resplendent body
Secondly, ensure her face is beautiful and lips are gorgeous
Now, prepare the sexy legs and add in the dazzling hair
Keep staring at her dazzling hair and enormous . . . eyes!
Then sparingly sprinkle the dark tan.
This mixture is extra special!
Try it yourself; I'm sure it'll work!

Jamie Dennis (13)
Hassenbrook School

The Recipe For A Perfect Family

There's a recipe for a family,
That's perfect, bold but true,
I haven't told a single soul,
So I'll tell you it from me to you.

First you need to mix,
Some kindness, smiles and spice,
And after that you need to add,
Some of your mum's homemade rice!

And then you need to add lots of love,
Not a sprinkle and not a drop,
Then mix, mix, mix,
No! Don't stop.

After that beat in a bit,
Of Dad, Mum and Sis,
And after that, maybe a bit of the dog,
Then whisk, whisk, whisk!

Then pop it in the oven,
At 360°, gas mark 4,
Bake until light brown and tanned,
And then shape and shape some more!

You should end up with,
A perfect tin of happy bliss,
So now all that's left is to thank your mum,
For helping with a big, wet, sloppy kiss!

Charlie Martin (12)
Hassenbrook School

Icing Of A Cake

I like the icing of a cake,
It's so hard and so light.
It doesn't look right without any icing,
It looks like a plain dried sponge.

Bradleigh Catmore (11)
Hassenbrook School

Incomplete

For every day in life,
There is a puzzle piece,
But at the end,
Few puzzles are complete.
Every time a sneer is passed on,
One puzzle piece is wasted,
Lost.

An evil person
By the name Bully,
Steals a piece daily,
Without right.

No matter how hard you try,
The bully will carry on.
No matter how hard you look,
The puzzle piece will not be found.
No matter how hard you wish,
The day cannot be relived.
Nothing can change that memory,
Therefore that piece will be lost forever.

That bully robs you of happiness,
That bully robs you of right,
That bully robs you of a puzzle piece.

No one can bring those pieces back,
But by replacing that sneer with a smile,
You can help someone,
Keep their remaining puzzle pieces.

Yet still life remains . . .
Incomplete.

Elinor Rew (13)
Hassenbrook School

Broken

Broken,
Left alone, hidden in the shadows.
Kept from the world.
Like a wilting flower,
Slowly turning from white to blood red.

Broken.
She falls to the ground,
As if a snowflake descends from above.
Her lifeless body lies limp upon the floor,
As her final breath leaves her.

Broken.
Standing over her,
She is now seen by the world.
They now see what they've done,
How she only lived half a life.

Broken.
Lying all alone.
The last nail goes in,
As the final rose hits the lid,
Guarding her for evermore.

Charlotte Dickinson (14)
Hassenbrook School

Raspberry Ice Cream

Ice cream is a shape of a cone,
The ice cream is my own,
The ice cream is sweet,
The ice cream is my treat,
My sister had a taste,
And got it over her face.

Amy Willson (11)
Hassenbrook School

A Thousand Years Of Darkness

The lightning roared like a ripping page,
The Lord above in an awful rage,
The men below, weighted by choice,
Cower in fear from His loud, vengeful voice,
The birds fly, fly far,
The fish disappear,
The world almost shatters,
Like the drums in the ears,
Darkness envelops the unsuspecting Earth,
While the Lord above continues to curse,
A thousand years pass,
The world left in tatters,
The Lord calms down,
And shuts His big gnashers,
The world is at peace, once more like before,
Until the next time,
The Lord rises . . . again.

James Bradley (13)
Hassenbrook School

Super Mind

I have a super mind
Pretty amazing and sublime
Always open like a book
Ready for me to take a look

I'm awake but in a dream
Dropping, falling but has no theme
Not noticing the surroundings
Sinking into the background looking at my foundings.

I'm not understanding
Still falling waiting for my landing.

Leeanna Davies (13)
Hassenbrook School

Anything Just To Make It Rhyme

I had a dream last night,
About this massive bright light,
In my dream there were my friends,
All rich in a Mercedes-Benz.

We were driving down the M25,
With the wind in our hair, we felt so alive,
We were playing music loud and clear,
So the whole of Essex could stand and hear.

About the light we saw,
It led to a house with a wooden door,
We knocked on the door that was alight,
So bright we hardly had any sense of sight.

The door opened with great effect,
Thunder and lightning we were thinking, *what the heck?*
We looked behind, the car was demolished,
It exploded, after we gave it this big, big polish.

We were disappointed, really mad,
That was the best car I ever had,
Anyway, we went through the door,
Kids playing footie, three-one was the score.

They were Japanese, playing every week,
There was one kid with two bruises on his cheek,
They asked us to play we gladly accepted,
They didn't want us to be lonely and rejected.

Ninety minutes, three-one at full time,
This poem was made up so that anything could rhyme,
For this last page I talked a load of rubbish,
What rhymes, what the hell, I'll just write 'fish'.

So here I go, I close my curtain,
I won't win this competition; I know that for certain,
So for my happiness please use mine,
This poem was made up so that anything could rhyme.

Chay Appleyard (14)
Hassenbrook School

My School

School is great
When you're not late
School is great
What's to hate?
The lessons
The teachers
The meals they feed ya.
School is great
Just me and my mates
Learning is fun
We dance and run
And do our sums
School is great
Just like my mates.

Danielle Thompson (12)
Hassenbrook School

Old School

Our
Lessons
Drone on
Every
Night and day

Dawns
Always
Yawning whilst

Scenic
Children
Hike
Over
Old
Land to
School.

Christopher Taylor-Webb (12)
Hassenbrook School

How To Make A Fit Boy

In order to make a yummy fit boy,
You will need the following special ingredients:

Firstly, you must take brown just-got-out-of-bed-look hair
And a lovely pair of big eyes, but the colour is unknown.
Secondly, ensure he has a mobile phone,
So he can text me when I'm alone.

Now prepare that cute little look,
So I can laugh and smile and stare for a while.

Gently fold in the fit and tanned bod
With a touch of the hand, a wink and a nod.

Also add a football!
Don't make him too tall.
I want him to be gorgeous, and not to be a fool.

Finally to ensure the mixture is tasty,
Add a pinch of sugar,
He'll be so cute he'll make all the girls go, *'Aahh!'*

This mixture is special, it's taste is unique,
This will make the nicest boy that you will ever meet.

Jade Hales (12)
Hassenbrook School

The Rainbow Full Of Mysteries

Up in the clouds
Lives a person, whose name is God
Every time it starts to pour bitter rain
God pulls the chain
A colourful rainbow forms, as bright as the sun
God starts to smile,
But there is always a man
With a loaded gun waiting to spoil the colours
He shoots
And the magic rainbow turns to blood.

Michael Ellis (13)
Hassenbrook School

Spotless

Long Gone John, with the bow tie in his hair,
Plays on a two-stringed fiddle for a penny,
Beneath the platform at Waterloo,
And thinks on tomorrow, but never yesterday.

Good Queen Luck of the daisy children,
Lies in a field of cornflower blue,
Singing of a time long since passed,
And weeping for dreams forgotten.

Odd Socked Maude, the departed child of grey,
Sits alone on doorstep, cold,
Chattering away to the coloured past,
And lamenting the years ahead.

These are the children of the past,
The lives of today,
The figments of the future.

These are the children of minds long lost,
These are those who do not think,
These are those missing from the world,
These are the spotless minds of forever.

Elizabeth Ebdale (14)
Hassenbrook School

My Idea Of Christmas

The presents all wrapped under the tree,
I look curiously, hoping some are for me.
I stare outside, hoping for snow,
As darkness falls, the Christmas lights glow.
The carol singers stand out in the cold,
Hoping for coins both silver and gold
This is my favourite time of year,
Listen, is that Santa's sleigh bells I hear?

Leya Pullen (12)
Hassenbrook School

Confusing Goodbyes

You said hello, then said goodbye
You told me you loved me
I don't know why.

I was your little girl
You always would say
I never did dream of a life
With you away.

Scattered tears
And scattered dreams
Are all you left me
So it seems.

A smile here
And a smile there
Is all you have to offer.

You said hello, then said goodbye
You told me you loved me
I don't know why.

Charlotte Cape (14)
Hassenbrook School

Why?

Why is a question that should always be asked,
Why is a question, just think of the past.

The past is a memory of good times and bad,
Through the pages of life, sometimes is sad.

But just think of the good times,
When life gets you down.

Think of the summer,
When nothing could get you down.

Then when you think your life is a bore,
Just think of the good things that have happened before.

Katharine Robson (13)
Hassenbrook School

At The End Of The Rainbow

At the end of the rainbow
What would be there?
Maybe some gold,
Or even a bear.

What's the colour
That comes first?
Red, blue or green
I think I might burst.

At the end of the rainbow
Everyone says it's great!
You may even make
A brand new mate.

What will be there
At the end of it all?
Maybe it's a great big
Shopping mall.

But then it'll be there
At the bottom of the tree
But what is there?
It's only me!

Natalie Gannon (13)
Hassenbrook School

How To Make A Friend

In order to make a good friend,
You will need the following:
Firstly you must take respect and politeness
The mixture should be tasty,
Secondly ensure it is sticky,
Now prepare the friendship,
Gently fold in the honesty,
And slowly stir in together,
Finally, to ensure the mixture is tasty,
Sprinkle in the kindness.

Jake Brindley (12)
Hassenbrook School

Great Minds

'Great minds think alike' my uncle said one day
But I don't believe that line that people commonly say.
How could a mind think the same?
Come on, it's just plain lame
No one can think the same
No way, it's insane!

So when your friends say the saying
Don't believe them and shout
'We can't think the same
It's inhumane!'

So when you're speaking to the queen
Don't believe her and scream
Do not say that line
Say . . .
'Your mind is much better than mine!'

Megan Potts (13)
Hassenbrook School

My Pet

I love my black cat
She is sweet and fat
When I see her playing on the path
She always makes me laugh
She looks like a bat
Running around for a gnat
Always wanting food
Can't give her any more, even though
She will get in a bad mood.

When I sleep at night
I like holding her tight
Her smooth black fur
I hear her purr
I love my pet
I'm glad we met.

Laura Bull (12)
Hassenbrook School

Winter/Christmas

When the nights are grey,
And snow falls all day.

When the birds all flee,
And the animals jump with glee.

When the leaves start to fall,
And the owls start to call.

When the wind turns bitter,
And the snow gets thicker.

When the Christmas tree is up,
And you have hot choc in a cup.

When shops get busy,
And parents get dizzy.

When you go to bed,
And find presents above your head.

Brodie Warren (12)
Hassenbrook School

Creeping Down The Corridor

Creeping down the corridor,
Checking, looking through each door.

Quick, here comes the janitor,
Hide in the classroom through the squeaky door.

Into the corridor I go again,
Looking behind then back again.

Creeping down the corridor,
Looking, checking through each door.

Turn right, y*es!* The playground door is in sight,
Having fun is on my mind.

Brring brring there goes the bell, just run,
'Luke, detention!' my teacher sang.

Luke Brown (12)
Hassenbrook School

Snowflake

Beautifully white,
Like stars in your eyes.
They never seem to break,
Until they hit the ground.

You always try to catch them
But they disappear in your hand.
Giving you a cold touch
On an early winter morning.

Each one unique
Like every one of us.
Just like people
In their own little way.

Always falling
Like angels from the heavens above.
In their moment of destiny.

Christopher Hatwell (14)
Hassenbrook School

I Want To Be Like The Queen

I want to be like the Queen,
Be rich and famous,
And rule the world,
My own kingdom is at my feet,
All the people I will get to meet,
My name will be heard all over this land,
'Have you heard of that Rebecca? She is so great!'
There will be no school or work;
My palace will be made of chocolate,
And I'll have servants and all time entertainers and cleaners
                                    and cooks.

I want to be like the Queen,
Why can't that be?

Rebecca Kirrane (13)
Hassenbrook School

I Like And I Don't Like!

I like hats,
But I don't like rats.

I like the rain
But it can also be a right pain.

I like shoes,
But I don't like to lose.

I like make-up,
But I don't like to wake up.

I like to share,
But I don't like Tony Blair.

I like presents,
But I don't like pheasants.

I like chips,
But I don't like ships.

I like my bed but . . .
I don't like my shed!

Keighley Weale (12)
Hassenbrook School

Love

Love is something you can't take
Love is something you can't break
Love is something true to you
That's why I believed in you.

Love can take you by surprise
Love can make you dry your eyes
Love can sometimes break your heart
You're better off being apart.

Love can sometimes be quite posh
Love is not about dosh
Wives are not here just to wash.

Tayla Wootton (12)
Hassenbrook School

Magical Feelings

A magical icy feeling,
With a soft, velvet touch.
Drifting from the sky,
A snowflake ready to die.

Love is in the air,
Shiny blood-red roses everywhere.
Hearts beating faster,
As your love comes closer.

Angels fall from above,
Making wishes come true.
As the sea starts to move;
The blood rushes through.

Hugs and kisses is all you want,
With a special magical feeling.
Happiness and love is everywhere,
Until your love is nowhere.

Hayley Bloomfield (14)
Hassenbrook School

Great Minds

Great minds
Plain minds
Exciting minds
Wacky minds
All our minds are different!

Animals have one,
Einstein had one,
We all have one,
Though they are all different.

Lorraine Smith (12)
Hassenbrook School

A Snowflake

A gleaming white substance,
Which flows through the air aimlessly.
It's called when the wind blows,
And begins to fall within an instant.

As it settles on the ground,
People watch in amazement.
Children cheer and scream,
As Christmas makes its appearance.

Snowmen and snowball fights,
Expressed ways of showing winter delight.
As adults stand and stare,
Children overjoyed, Santa is near.

Christmas morning, presents for all,
A great sight to behold.
Snowflakes continue to descend from the sky,
Everyone enjoy the Christmas holiday.

Luke Jordan (15)
Hassenbrook School

Phat Friends

In order to make a 'phat' friend,
You will need to get the following special ingredients:
Firstly you must have a normal person and really phat clothes,
The mixture should look like a basketball player mixed with a genius,
Secondly, ensure the right footwear, preferably Air Jordan's,
Gently fold in the silky skills,
And slowly stir together the fancy footwork,
Finally, to ensure the mixture is great
Sparingly sprinkle the contents of a growbag,
This mixture is special, it will be unique,
This will be with you for all your life to help you along the way.

George Crudgington (12)
Hassenbrook School

How To Make A Perfect Parent

In order to make a perfect parent,
You will need the following special ingredients:
Firstly, you must take some snazzy clothes and lots of money,
The mixture should be runny like honey,
Secondly, ensure the look is perfect,
Now prepare the loving smile.
Gently fold in the pushover personality
And slowly stir together the warm mixture.
Finally, to ensure the mixture is tasty,
Sparingly sprinkle a fashionable dress sense.
This mixture is perfect
It tastes unique.
Enjoy your new perfect parent!

Danielle Walker (12)
Hassenbrook School

How To Make A Rainbow

In order to make a rainbow
You will need some very special ingredients:
You must start with some happiness
And a tablespoon of smiles.
The mixture should now be sunny enough
To pour into a bowl of colours.
Secondly you must scoop it together into a bundle of joy.
Gently fold in some happy friendship,
And sprinkle on some love.
This mixture is powerful and great for everyone.
It will bring this world some much needed sun.

Caroline Stoten (12)
Hassenbrook School

Snowflakes And Roses

One of these shows the sparkle of spring,
The other a glimmer of winter,
But both are a beautiful thing.

One of these falls from the sky,
The other falls from the earth,
But they both make you feel high.

One covers the earth in a sheet of white,
The other a sheet of red,
But they are both a wonderful sight.

The first is a snowflake,
The other a rose,
But both of them; what dreams they make.

Michael Smith (14)
Hassenbrook School

Cavemen

The first inventors of our time,
They discovered fire and the wheel,
They learnt what to eat and what not to eat,
They hunted with home-made weapons,
They survived in caves with none of our comforts.

The men and women then were not as smart as us, but,
They had kept our race alive,
They had begun our evolution,
Without them, we would not be here today.

To me they were great minds,
The great minds of the past.

Isla Montgomery (12)
Hassenbrook School

How To Make A Special Friend

In order to make a special friend,
You will need the following special ingredients:
Firstly you must take a cutie pie smile and broad blue eyes.
The mixture should be soft.
Secondly ensure the blonde hair is smooth.
Now, prepare the bubbly personality,
Gently fold in the cheeky attitude
And slowly stir together the cool appearance.
Finally, to ensure the mixture is tasty,
Sparingly sprinkle some bright, colourful clothes.
This mixture is special,
Its taste unique,
Now you can dip your new friend in a bundle of treats.

Lauren Weaver (13)
Hassenbrook School

Roses

They come in white but mostly in red,
People throw down the petals when you're dead,
They touch people in many different ways,
People love them until the end of their days,
In the summer, a wonderful sight,
All the colours, oh so bright,
When they die, the petals fall like snow,
Until spring returns again when they re-grow.
Those flowers are brilliant, I suppose.
That wonderful, wonderful, wonderful rose.

James Hawkridge (14)
Hassenbrook School

When A Woman's Made Her Mind Up

I'm standing in front of the mirror
Thinking, *damn,* to myself
I should've known the time would come
When she would find somebody else

All those good times
All my poems and my rhymes
All my gifts and the things I let her permanently borrow
Now all I'm left with, is a heart full of sorrow

When a woman's made her mind up
No matter how much you beg
She'd rather stick with that guy instead
She'll neglect your feelings
And leave your heart bleeding

Forever is how long you promised me your heart
But I know you were lying, straight from the start

Beautiful, that's one of the things you are
But you're his by far
Watching you and him,
Hoping that it would soon be me holding you that way
Hoping all day long, all my free time I pray

It hurts knowing that we'll never be
All this crazy stuff, it doesn't make sense to me
You say you don't like poems it's not the way to your heart
You say it wouldn't work out, you say it from the start

So now I'm standing here holding my rose
Hurtfully knowing he's the one that you chose.

Christopher Wilson (14)
Hassenbrook School

An Angel's Tear

A beautiful angel sits alone in the heavens above
Looking down on a wonderful world
As peaceful as a dove
A tear falls from her eye
My pain is making her cry
I wish I could stop her fears
I would wipe her snowflake tears
That she weeps
As a tear falls from Heaven
It forms into a frozen raindrop
As soft as skin
As white as white
As cold as ice
Falls so gently
From the grey midnight sky
So next time it snows
Now you know
Those frozen little raindrops
Are really tears falling from the sky
Falling from an angel's eye.

Tania Fuller (14)
Hassenbrook School

Snowflake From Heaven

A snowflake is a signal from Heaven
Letting us all know the beauty the world possesses.
Each snowflake is like a falling star, shining its beauty afar.
They fall as gentle as a pillow and grace the ground beneath
Giving it life and light at dark times.
It is a crystal falling from the sky a white glint from up high.
It follows a path of wind just like a dream of mine.

Anthony Lock (15)
Hassenbrook School

A Pessimist's View

Some see the world as a blessing,
I can see a curse,
Some see the world progressing,
I can see the reverse.

The glass is half empty,
It's not half full.
You might prefer to push,
But I'm going to pull.

Is it the sun or is it the moon?
Is it day or is it night?
Well, even in the afternoon,
I stand under the light of the moon.

What's wrong with you fools,
Are you blind?
The world is vicious and cruel,
Not at all kind.

Opinions may come
Opinions may go,
But I'm certain of what I know.
Optimism is a false reality,
Filled with lies and fake hospitality.

It's a crime against all humanity
To believe in this insanity,
Our lives are struggles just to stay alive,
Because at any time we could fall down and die.

I hate the hopefulness
And people's positive opinions
To hell with the optimists
And ignore their opinions!

Melissa Godman (14)
Hassenbrook School

A Field

A field in summer is full of gleam,
This field is where roses are seen,
A rose, an erect thorny shrub,
A scented, motley blossom,
But when in winter, the field is full of glow,
To see it full of pure white snow,
And just above a graceful, drifting snowflake can be seen,
A snowflake, a single, small, feathery duster,
Of crystals, of glaciated water vapour,
Now in spring the snow has melted away,
The field is where seeds are being laid.

Samantha Corker (14)
Hassenbrook School

In The Snow

As the twinkling star falls through the air
It shines like a diamond.
Twinkles of frost glimmer on velvety petals.
The magical smell runs through the cold air.
Everything is covered in fluffy white snow.
Different shapes of crystal fall to the floor
And slowly their shapes melt into a cold puddle of water.
Footsteps in the snow dig deep into the floor
And they slowly fill up once again with the glittering stars.

Bethany Clark (14)
Hassenbrook School

How To Make A Devil

To make a devil,
You will need these dark materials,
To start you must take pure evil and pour in hot water,
This mixture must be wet and murky,
Next you must put in a hairy forked tail,
Now you must prepare the mixture by stirring with a devil's fork,
Then you must pour in the blood of five pure evil people
To complete the mixture you must sprinkle fire over the mixture.
This mixture is special
It makes a devil.

Simon Robinson (12)
Hassenbrook School

Teacher Recipe

When you make a brilliant teacher
The following is required:
A chunk of humour and a teaspoon of brain,
The mixture should be runny.
Secondly add personality to ensure the mixture's smooth,
Prepare the main ingredient which is the lesson plan.
Fold in the heart to make it strong,
Now slowly stir together the concoction.
Finally sprinkle with detentions (to keep the horrors at bay),
This is how to make a brilliant teacher.

Grant Robinson (12)
Hassenbrook School

Happy Now - But Looking Back

Happy now - but looking back,
Looking back into those trenches of torture,
Hoping guns won't shoot.
Many friends already dead.
Whose turn is it next to go up above?
No one knows.

Happy now - but looking back,
Looking back to the times we fought for survival.
Thinking of our families - will we see them again?
And if we do, will we walk or talk?
Will we be too injured to move?
No one knows.

Looking back - but happy now.
We have survived - well, some of us have.
Now at home in the warmth of our families,
With our full fridges and freezers.
How long will we have left?
No one knows!

Emily Eversden (11)
Honywood School

Gone

She woke, strings held up her arms.
If they were to break, she would fall onto her palms.
A white dress laid upon her body a halo upon her head.
She floated around a little boy's room weeping because she's dead.
A scream was let out, she was gone.
As she left she hummed a song.
Some say she cut her strings and was let free,
Some say she flew away not knowing where she'd be.

Danielle Bugbee (11)
Honywood School

My Head Teacher

My head teacher was once a baby
My head teacher owned teddy bears
My head teacher was stroppy, slammed doors
Lost his temper, stomped up the stairs

My head teacher stole the biscuits
My head teacher threw his food
My head teacher was sent to his bedroom
He was told that he was rude.

My head teacher went to secondary school
My head teacher's top button was undone
My head teacher got detention, was naughty
He thought it was a load of fun.

My head teacher is my head teacher now
My head teacher wears suits and a tie
My head teacher teaches us to be good
Such naughty things he'd deny.

Poppy Gerrard-Abbott (11)
Honywood School

Mary

My friend Mary,
She's quite hairy,
And when she gets wet she looks very scary,
Though she's really very nice,
She always eats my rice,
And when we have the chocolate cake she gets the biggest slice!
Mary's a gorilla,
You really have to see her,
But she'll be back to the zoo if she doesn't learn to use the loo!

Laura Lydford (11)
Honywood School

Pens

Gel pens,
Smelly pens,
Pens without any lids.

Berol pens,
Calligraphy pens,
Pens which are meant for kids.

Highlighter pens,
Rollerball pens,
Pens which are good from the start.

Felt-tip pens,
Colour ink pens,
Pens which are good for art.

Pens, pens, all shapes and sizes,
Coloured or not,
They're full of surprises.

Katie Watts (11)
Honywood School

Science

Body organs
Body parts
All with a different job
Helping you live and stay alive
Body organs
Body parts
Cells like rooms
Organs like houses
Helping you move and stretch.

Katie Parker (11)
Honywood School

Rainy Day

Pitter-patter,
Pitter-patter
Running off my nose,
Pitter-patter,
Pitter-patter,
Landing on my toes!

Running off the rooftop,
Falling to the mud,
Racing down the windows,
Landing with a thud.

Splashing in the puddles,
Flicking up the grit
Dancing through the raindrops,
Onto the house to sit.

Putting on my wellies,
Opening up the door,
Few steps outside,
It's raining even more!

Time to go inside,
I'm getting cold and wet,
Not to worry now it's slowing,
It's stopping now I bet.

Pitter-patter,
Pitter-patter,
Running off my nose,
Pitter-patter,
Pitter-patter,
Splashing on my toes.

Ella Neale (12)
Honywood School

Truly Special

I felt terrible
My head hurt
My stomach hurt
My legs hurt
Everything hurt.

Lots of tests
Eye tests
Hearing tests
MRI tests
Blood tests
Breathing tests
X-ray tests
When will it end?

'TB, Meningitis,' they said
Mum and Dad were terrified.
I just felt sick
Sick all the time.

Slowly I got better
And went to the hospital school.
After three months I came home.

But it was different.
I was different.
I was full of medicine
But I couldn't see or balance,
I wasn't really me.

I went to a special school
But I wanted to be the same.
I was angry with the world
Why me?

Now I'm older I understand
That it really is alright to be me
And that I am really
Truly special.

Katie Gardner (11)
Honywood School

My Dog Bengi

When I'm feeling down and really sad
I think of my dog Bengi and that thought makes me glad.

When I see Bengi and how he reacts to me,
I feel really happy and want to jump around with glee.

Being woken up in the morning by him jumping on my bed
And him falling to sleep next to me after being fed.

The thought of my dog Bengi jumping on my bed
Makes me feel happy in the head!

Sam Steele (11)
Honywood School

What If . . .

What would it be like if . . .
I was a bird
Soaring through the sky
Watching everything that happens
Out of the corner of my eye
Landing on a rooftop
Singing out loud?
My friends could come and join me
And make me feel proud.

During the day
Searching for food
Go back to the nest
In a joyful mood
I eat my food
I fall asleep
What would it be like if . . .
I was a bird.

Rachel Wright (13)
Sanders Draper School

The Snow

I woke up one morning, to get ready to go,
But then I looked out of the window and saw the white snow,
I went outside and the school was closed!
It was all snowy, it had froze.

I rang my friends to see if they had the same sight,
They said, 'Yes!' I said, 'Snowball fight!'
I chucked on some clothes and rushed out of the door,
I immediately fell over, because of the icy floor.

I went inside, I had broken my toe,
I had to go upstairs and not enjoy the snow,
So on that day, I never got to play,
So I'll save my winter clothes for another day.

Sam Wickens (12)
Sanders Draper School

Bricks Have Feelings Too

What would it be like if I was a brick?
Being hit with balls
And kids being sick,
Holding up a house and surviving many falls.

Bricks are always treated
With not an inch of respect,
Think what it would be like, if we didn't have them,
No strong houses and hospitals too.

So, next time that you see a brick,
Just take a look at it,
Don't just take the mick,
After all, it's just a brick.

Michael Ayers (12)
Sanders Draper School

The Beslan Siege

What is it like to be a child stuck inside?
Nowhere for them to run, nowhere to hide,
Who were they to run to? No one was in sight.
Some were thinking, how could I have stopped the fight?

Stuck in the corner, trying to be still,
If not, the rebels would start to kill.
Trying to be positive and strong,
But how could they? They knew they were wrong.

All they have inside them is fears,
Imagine all the families with eyes of tears.
Are they dead or are they alive?
Would they cope and would they survive?

Just think of what they must feel,
For us it is imagining, for them it is real!

Leanne Briggs (12)
Sanders Draper School

Swimming

What it would be like if I were a professional swimmer,
I'd glide along like a winner,
Swimming breaststroke through the day,
Earning medals along the way.

Doing front crawl in a race,
Splashing water at my face,
Running round and round,
Lying worn out, on the ground.

Winning medals all day long,
Counting the lengths whilst I go along,
Talking and playing with my friends,
Hoping the day never ends.

Claire Wilson (12)
Sanders Draper School

I Wonder . . .

I wonder what it is like to be an angel in the sky?
Why don't they come out and say hello?
I wonder if they are shy?

I wonder what it is like to be a beautiful, shining star?
Why are they out in space?
Why are they out so far?

I wonder what it is like to be a bird flying high?
How I would like to be a bird
Soaring through the sky.

I wonder what it is like to be a little, fluffy bunny?
To eat, sleep and play all day,
I bet it would be funny!

I wonder what it is like to be a beautiful celebrity?
To go around shopping all day
And eating cakes with tea.

I wonder what it is like to be a child who is disabled?
For everywhere you go in the world,
You will always be labelled.

I wonder what it is like to be a person in Iraq?
To walk the streets every day
And have to watch your back.

I wonder what it is like to be a wounded, tortured slave?
You would not be allowed to have fun,
You must not misbehave.

I wonder what it is like to have no family that have survived?
To have no one to love you
Or stand by your side.

I wonder what it is like to be a child who is very lucky?
I don't have to wonder anymore,
Because that child is me!

Grace Sussex (13)
Sanders Draper School

I Wonder . . .

I wonder what it's like to be a fighter,
Like Muhammed Ali?
I wonder what it's like to float
Like a butterfly and sting like a bee?
I wonder what it's like to be
Wayne Rooney on TV?
I wonder what it's like to be a monkey
Swinging from tree to tree?
I wonder what it's like to be a 90-year-old,
An OAP?
I wonder what it's like to be Jimmy Riddle,
Playing a fiddle?
I wonder what it's like to be a bird,
Flying free?
I wonder what it's like to be a fish
In the sea?
I wonder what it's like to be sitting
In a very tall tree?
I wonder what it's like to be standing,
Like a Christmas tree?

Robert Clark (13)
Sanders Draper School

I Wonder What It Would Be Like To Be . . .

I wonder what it would be like to be a bird?
To spread my wings and just fly away,
Each and every single day,
To fly wherever and whenever,
The wind gliding through my feathers.

I wonder what it would be like to watch a baby bird hatch?
To sit in my nest, a perfect patch.
Eating worms night and day
And when I want to, just fly away . . .

Laura Martin (14)
Sanders Draper School

I Wonder What It's Like To Be . . .

I wonder what it's like to be invisible for a day?
Follow everyone and see what they say,
Jump behind people and give them a scare,
They pretend to be brave, like they don't care.

I wonder what it's like to be a pencil in a tin?
Dark and dingy when no one looks in,
When someone's feeling artistic, they pick me from the others
And then they get bored, so they hide me under the covers.

I wonder what it's like to be a photo in a book?
Be complimented and criticised when people take a look,
No one can be bothered, so it sits on a shelf,
Sad and lonely, all by itself.

I wonder what it's like to be anything in the world?
Short, long, thick, thin, straight or even curled,
You could be a plane, a lamp or even a word,
A bag, a table, a tropical bird.

Louise Wood (14)
Sanders Draper School

Jungle

I wonder what it's like to be a monkey swinging from tree to tree?
People gather from here and there
To stare at me with glee.

I wonder what it's like to be a man wearing a loin cloth?
It's cooling in every weather,
I wonder if it is eaten by moths?

I wonder what it's like to be a grapevine hanging from a tree?
Swinging back and forth all day,
Maybe swinging above the sea.

Sammy Foot (13)
Sanders Draper School

I Wonder . . .

I wonder what it's like to be,
A millionaire living in glee,
Driving around in flash, posh cars,
Knowing every man would marry me?

I wonder what it's like to be,
A homeless child living in vain,
Just sitting there in agony,
No life, no family, just full of pain?

I wonder what it's like to be,
A star up in the dark night sky?
Twinkle here, twinkle there, twinkle on me,
In comes the morning, as if they've just died.

I wonder what it's like to be,
Someone special and full of fun?
They'd dance all night until the morning bright,
Because that special person is me!

Funmike Meheux (13)
Sanders Draper School

Iraq

What is it like to be a child in Iraq?
At least we can go to the park
The children there, don't go to school
They must think it's rather cool
The children in Iraq cannot play
As they have to have a working day
The children should be having fun
Not being held up by a gun
Children blindfolded, children dead
Who will rest their poor, little heads?
All the children should be free
Just like they want to be.

Simon Apen-Sadler (13)
Sanders Draper School

The Beslan Siege

What is it like to be a hostage?
Scared and cannot move,
Only a child,
A whole life to live.

No food or water,
No fans to cool you down,
No parents to wipe your tears,
Only criminals to kill you.

Bombs near you, next to you,
Everywhere you look,
Try not to move,
It will only kill you faster.

So hot, can't open the window,
Can only take your clothes off,
But it does not cool you.

After all the pain and killings,
After all the times you thought you would die,
Somebody comes to rescue you,
It's about time.

Worried mums and dads,
Waiting outside,
You can see all the tears in their eyes,
Happy that you have survived.

The people get you out,
The worrying has gone,
Running to your parents,
You have survived!

Bethany Harnwell (12)
Sanders Draper School

I Wonder What It's Like To Be . . .

I wonder what it's like to be,
My bed that is so snug all day?
It doesn't walk or talk like me,
But still feels me up with glee?

I wonder what it's like to be,
A homeless person on the streets,
With no food and with no money?
The only hope is it will be sunny.

I wonder what it's like to be,
A prisoner so far from free,
To try to escape from metal cuffs,
It should be hard but not for me?

I wonder what it's like to be,
An Eskimo by the sea,
Ice all around and for a home?
It seems cold, but keeps me warm.

I wonder what it's like to be,
A scientist going crazy,
Of what he's made and what he's done?
To me it would not be fun.

I wonder what it's like to be,
A mum who is the mother of three,
One pretty girl and two horrid boys,
Who have too many annoying toys?

I wonder what it's like to be,
A dolphin swimming in the sea,
No boundaries to restrict her,
Able to swim where no one goes?

Elisabeth Mann (13)
Sanders Draper School

Wonder What It's Like . . .

What is it like to live in Iraq?
The never-ending bombs
And terrorists, all in black,
They all fear to turn their backs.
You feel weary of all the cars,
Then you hear a bang and heat on your face,
Your friends have just been killed,
The sorrow, the sorrow.

What is it like to live in Iraq?
You don't know what to do,
You're scared it could be you next,
There is nowhere to run or go,
The terror is all around you,
Searching for new victims,
You will never escape it,
There is nothing you can do.

What is it like to live in Iraq?
People die for what they think is right,
That is what a terrorist is like,
Don't care or bother for anyone
And don't really care what they've done,
So they're dead and asleep in their final bed
And that is what it's like to live in Iraq.

Scott Tuffey (13)
Sanders Draper School

Flying

Imagine flying through the sky,
Through the clouds and going high,
Swooping, soaring, wind blowing in your face,
Speeding in rows like you're having a race,
Sparrow, blue tit, blackbird, thrush,
All flying high in a rush,
Bullfinch, starling, rook, magpie,
Into the setting sun they fly.

Nathan Bull (12)
Sanders Draper School

I Wonder?

I wonder what it's like to be a fox?
Being hunted every day,
Running into your home,
Hoping the dogs won't come.

I used to have a fox as a friend,
She used to come into my garden,
Until her life came to an end.
She gave birth to cubs behind the shed,
Then one night came Fred,
The killer fox,
Who killed all the cubs,
My friend ran away,
With no defence,
Where did she go? I don't know,
But she never came back again.

I heard on the news, foxhunting might be banned,
I shouted, *hooray!* with joy,
Now all foxes would have peace,
No dogs chasing them,
Getting bitten and left to die,
I wonder what it's like to be a fox . . .
I wonder?

Sammy Hills (12)
Sanders Draper School

What Is It Like To Be . . .

What is it like to be a cat,
When you have to sleep on a mat?

What is it like to be a teacher,
When you have to act like a preacher,
Keeping all your bad thoughts in your head
And saying it to the staff instead?

What is it like to be a lion,
When you have the ground to lie on?

Elizabeth Fashanu (11)
Sanders Draper School

What's It Like To Be A Drug User?

What's it like to be a drug user,
When every day's a struggle,
When life is just a blur,
Like you're in a cloudy bubble?

Nothing can get through
And nothing can get out,
You want to stop and change,
You want to scream and shout.

The drugs have a hold on you,
They control everything in your life,
You think they make you happy,
But they scare you like a knife!

And maybe you feel great,
But you never can be sure,
Because life's like a strange dream
And all you want is more.

People stop and stare,
I sometimes wonder why,
They look at me like I'm a freak,
That's when I want to cry.

I feel the drugs eating at me,
Turning my brain to mush,
But I feel like I need them,
I crave that weird rush.

I'm hoping it will end . . .
That the pains will go away,
But no one can help me now,
My night will never turn to day.

Ryan Burnett (13)
Sanders Draper School

What Is It Like To Be In The Beslan Siege?

What is it like to be in the Beslan siege?
I know, I was there.
I could hear screams all around me,
I wanted to hold them and let them be.
I saw blood all around me
And thought of my brother,
But I knew he was killed by another.
They took all my clothes,
Until I was bare,
But I was too frightened to care.
They spat on us like we were scum,
I prayed and prayed that someone would come.
I could hear my mother calling for me,
I wondered if I would ever be free?
The creature came towards me and told me to bow,
But I promised to be brave, that was a vow.
He spat in my beaten face,
I closed my eyes in disgrace.
Suddenly, he trod on my back
And placed a gun at my head
And it hit me that soon I would be dead.
I felt some fear,
For death to be so near.
Five, four, three, two, one.
Bam!
I was killed by a gun.

Ella Williams (12)
Sanders Draper School

I Wonder What It's Like To Be A Bird?

I wonder what it's like to be a bird?
To fly around in the sky all day,
Gliding in the sun's rays,
Eating worms in the morning,
Getting up when the day is dawning.

I wonder what it's like to build a nest?
The twigs I use, have got to be the best,
To lay my eggs in my home,
Don't want to leave the chicks too long on their own.

I wonder what it's like to sit in the trees?
To come and go as I please,
To hide amongst all the leaves,
Try not to fall in the breeze.

I wonder what it's like to fly in the air with the clouds?
To spread my wings and follow the crowd,
To go somewhere else when it gets cold, would be great,
Get in formation, don't want to be late!

Daniel Ridley (13)
Sanders Draper School

I Wonder . . .

I wonder what it's like to be an Olympic gold medal winner,
Welcomed back home with crowds cheering and praising me?
I wonder what it's like to be an excellent singer,
Performing on stage at Wembley Arena filling with glee.
I wonder what it's like to be a Sunday roast dinner,
Would I feel like drowning in that deep gravy sea?
I wonder what it's like to be a Formula 1 racing driver,
Maybe I could beat Michael Schumacher and drive his Ferrari?

I wonder what it's like to be the person reading this,
Trapped inside their head, surrounded by a vast abyss?

Chantelle Carter (13)
Sanders Draper School

I Wonder What It's Like To Be . . .

I wonder what it's like to be,
A plane going around the planet,
A girl having just thrown up and her name is Janet?
I wonder what it's like to be,
A chocolate in a box,
People never able to choose out of all us chocs?
I wonder what it's like to be,
A fish on a plate?
All I have to do is wait.
I wonder what it's like to be,
High up on a tree,
Me and the rest of my family?
I wonder what it's like to be,
A carrot sitting on a plate
And me and a broccoli on a date?
I wonder what it's like to be,
A dog sleeping on the floor,
Never having any chores?
I wonder what it's like to be.
A copper going around schools,
Always getting lost on their way to the halls?

Jennifer Alderslade (11)
Sanders Draper School

Homeless

What is it like to be an elderly, homeless woman?
Too poor to eat and drink healthily,
Sleeping rough out on the streets,
Having no family to care,
Searching for scraps so you can live,
Seeing people on the streets with family all around them,
Being able to eat and drink without worry,
What is it like to be an elderly, homeless woman?
Well, pretty tough to me.

Jessica Rix (12)
Sanders Draper School

What Is It Like To Be . . .

What is it like to be,
In that siege?
What is it like to see,
Your friends and teachers murdered in cold blood?
What is it like to think,
Your school will have an insurrection?
What is it like to be,
Surrounded by merciless terrorists?
What is it like to see,
A gun pointed at you?
What is it like,
To think you're never going home?
What is it like to be,
Shot and left for dead?

Adam Spilsbury (12)
Sanders Draper School

I Wonder What It Is Like To Be . . .

What is it like to be a person who lives on the streets?
How would you feel if you sat there day by day
Watching people walk past you, as you beg for money?
How would you feel if you had to go through bins for food?
How would you feel if people laughed and kicked you
As they walked past?
How would you feel without a house,
No friends and no fun?
How would you feel if people took the mick out of you
As they walked past?
How would you feel if you lay there each night
Looking up at the sky, thinking what happened to you,
As you cried yourself to sleep?
Then the next morning, you think that you have to go through that slow,
Horrible day again and again and again.

Daniel Haywood (13)
Sanders Draper School

I Wonder What It Is Like To Be . . .

I wonder what it's like to be a tiger in the jungle?
And what it's like to sit in trees and frighten all the bees?
Then I go, let me show you, what I do . . .
Roar, roar, roar, roar, roar, roar.
Look up here, it's me,
Roar, roar, roar, roar, roar, roar
Listen to the rustle in the trees.

I wonder what it's like to be a carrot in a stew?
While people eat me, when they have the flu.

I wonder what it's like to be a kite?
Flying right up in the air with all my might.

I wonder what it's like to be a fruit?
With people looking at me as if I am cute.

I wonder what it's like to be a pen?
Being held by all the ugly men.

Daniella Green (12)
Sanders Draper School

I Wonder What It Is Like To Be . . .

I wonder what it is like to be,
A football being kicked about?
I really hope that I don't create a shout.

I wonder what it's like to be,
A bird gliding through the sky,
Searching for worms for my evening pie?

I wonder what it's like to be,
A giraffe so tall, reaching out to space,
My legs running, sprinting at an incredible pace?

I wonder what it's like to be,
A mirror gleaming at somebody's back?
Oh no! Please do not turn around,
You'll make the mirror crack!

Ope Ore (11)
Sanders Draper School

This Is The World We Live In

I wonder what it is like to be living in a family,
Where your mum gets bullied by your dad?
You have no control over it
And you wish all the hurt would stop.

I wonder what it is like to be held hostage,
Knowing you're going to be killed,
But also knowing you can be freed,
Wishing you weren't there?

I wonder what it is like to go to bed every night,
Hearing bombs and gunfire, hoping it will all stop and be over?
And then you hear the door being banged down,
Your mum screams . . . *bang!*

I wonder what it is like to be living on the streets,
Begging for money that no one gives you,
Having nowhere to go,
Wishing you hadn't run away from home,
Seeing happy people and then the sinking, guilty feeling appears?

I wonder what it is like to be all of these people,
Knowing no one will help you,
Having to live with yourself, for not doing the right thing,
Or dying on the cold, icy ground?

Katie Fox (13)
Sanders Draper School

I Wonder What It's Like To Be . . .

I wonder what it's like to be,
A poster and the things that I would see,
Everyone picking their noses
And putting it all on me?

I wonder what it's like to be,
A woman doing all the work around the house
And being afraid of little things,
Little things like a mouse?

Joe Shelden (11)
Sanders Draper School

What Is It Like To Be Abused?

What is it like to be abused?
Waiting, terrified for your life.
The footsteps of the attacker,
Coming, maybe with a knife.

The pain of the bruises and the cuts,
Like a dagger in your heart.
The upset and the misery
And that is just the start.

As the hands of time are turning,
With every tick-tock in your head.
The hands on him are beating,
You wish you were dead.

If only you could tell the truth,
Your life could not be worse.
There must be some way to stop this hurt
And end the painful curse.

Your life would be so simple then,
All pain and fear would cease.
A childhood everyone deserves,
Of love, safety and peace.

Amy Munro (13)
Sanders Draper School

What's It Like To Be An Orphan?

O n my own in my room
R unning around frantically
P eople stare and turn their nose up
H unting for every crumb
A nywhere I go
N o one stops to help
S o what's it like to be an orphan?

Emma Tucker (13)
Sanders Draper School

I Wonder What It Is Like To Be . . .

I wonder what it is like to be,
A millionaire swimming in a pool of money,
Go down the shop for a house
And not a jar of honey?

I wonder what it is like to be,
A carrot, being a vegetable,
Picked from the ground,
Eaten, never again being useable.

I wonder what it is like to be,
A bar of soap smelling fresh,
Being run out,
Praying for hope?

I wonder what it is like to be,
A baby doing poos,
Being sick maybe?

I wonder what it is like to be,
A piece of chewing gum stuck in the mouth of Louise,
Going down the shop and saying to the shopkeeper,
'Can I have some chewing gum, please?'

Evan Burrows (12)
Sanders Draper School

If Everyone Was Happy

What it would be like if everyone was happy?
Eight o'clock morning news,
Innocent person dead, because the killer was on booze,
As the police put up the yellow tape,
It could be another rape.

Criminals get away with some of their crimes committed,
Only some who get caught will admit it,
If the human race prevented these things from happening,
The world would be a better place.

Laura Jefferson (12)
Sanders Draper School

Wonder What It Is Like To Be . . .

I wonder what it is like to be,
An apple growing on a tree,
Green and red,
Hanging free?

I wonder what it is like to be,
A goldfish swimming with glee,
My brothers and sisters following me
And only a two second memory?

I wonder what it is like to be,
A frog leaping from a lillypad,
High in the sky, my tongue out high,
Eating flies, with bulging eyes?

I wonder what it is like to be,
A bird flying high in the sky,
Perching on the trees,
With doves following me?

I wonder what it is like to be,
A lobster soaring in the sea,
Clipping my claws
At everyone I see?

Ryan Harris (11)
Sanders Draper School

The Crow

It lurks around in sight of rats
It's very sneaky, like a cat
But when a human is near
The crow will flee in fear.

It shouts out its horrific screech
That will scare anything in sight
It is ruthless at the dead of night
When it comes out to fight.

Tom Smee (11)
Sanders Draper School

I Wonder What It's Like To Be . . .

I wonder what it's like to be,
A cat, eating my favourite food all day,
Getting lost in the trees all day,
Or playing with my friends, hooray!

I wonder what it's like to be,
A fish swimming in the sea,
Jumping around and shimmering,
My brothers, sisters and me?

I wonder what it's like to be,
A mirror sitting on the wall all day,
Not knowing what I look like,
When people go away?

I wonder what it's like to be,
A sofa, tall and comfy
And humming a tiny, quiet,
Little sofa song?

I wonder what it's like to be,
A snowflake, cold and falling from the sky,
Looking down on everyone,
From way up high?

I wonder what it's like to be,
A tree standing tall and strong?
I'm wooden and brown,
I never wear a frown.

I wonder what it's like to be,
A flower so colourful and fun,
Standing around all day
In the summer sun?

I wonder what it's like to be,
A firework being shot into the air?
Not living long,
But I don't care.

I wonder what it's like to be,
A TV being switched on all day?
I'd like to get up one day
And play.

I wonder what it's like to be,
A grape sitting and able to play?
Getting put into someone's mouth,
It's the end of my day.

Emily Butler (11)
Sanders Draper School

I Wonder . . .

I wonder what it's like to be a ghost,
Wandering around, discovering new things,
Picking them up while people stare,
Screaming cos there's no one there?

I wonder what it's like to be a star,
Up so high with the moon,
Shining and gleaming for everyone to see?
Oh look, everyone look at me.

I wonder what it's like to be the moon,
A big, shining thing up in the sky,
Sending a glow down to Earth,
Shining down on you and I?

I wonder what it's like to be a balloon,
To be blown up and hung on a wall,
That piece of rubber with air inside,
Hanging, just waiting to be popped?

I wonder what it's like to be a celebrity,
With all that money and glamour,
To go wherever you want and always get noticed?
It must be a wonderful life.

But there we go, it's all just thoughts,
But maybe, someday, we will all know what it's like to be a . . .

Jenna James (14)
Sanders Draper School

I Wonder What It Is Like To Be A . . .

I wonder what it is like to be,
A flower blooming in the sun,
Not even able to run?

I wonder what it is like to be,
A monkey climbing from tree to tree?
That would be me.

I wonder what it is like to be,
A bird sleeping in my nest,
Not disturbing and not being a pest?

I wonder what it is like to be,
A mirror, beautiful and bright?
Don't look at me,
Otherwise I'll get a terrible fright.

I wonder what it is like to be,
A cloud looking down at people?
Oh look at that crowd!

Shallece Bernard (11)
Sanders Draper School

I Wonder What It Is Like To Be . . .

I wonder what it is like to be a spider,
People scared of you
And trying to whack you with a newspaper?

I wonder what it is like to be a lion,
Roaring and chasing other animals?

I wonder what it is like to be a bat,
Flying and hunting in the darkness?

I wonder what it is like to be a snake,
Slithering and gliding around?

I wonder what it is like to be a bee,
Buzzing to every plant, one by one?

Nicholas Metcalfe (11)
Sanders Draper School

What's It Like To Be Abused?

I sit in my room, scared as any child in this situation would be,
What will happen next?
Will all this hitting stop?
Will we end up as a happy family?
My face is like a balloon ready to pop!
I want to tell someone, I really do,
But who?

It will just make the pain worse,
He will get angry and hit her again.
I don't want to let her go through that,
My body is aching, my face abused,
What will the children say at school
When they see me bruised?
Will they laugh, will they be scared for me?
My bruises are as black as the night's sky.

I love my family and always will,
Like any normal child would.
Sounds silly, I know!
Just think, when you're in your house,
With nothing worrying you, think,
What's it like to be abused?

Charlotte Watts (13)
Sanders Draper School

Christmas

Christmas is a time to be jolly
Everywhere decorated in mistletoe and holly
Children playing with their new toys
Sweets getting munched by girls and boys
Snow settling on the ground
Carol singing, a pleasant sound
White blankets of snow
Colourful houses seem to glow
Sitting in the corner, a beautiful tree
Everybody seems to be full of glee.

Rebecca Harris (13)
Sanders Draper School

What's It Like To Be Disabled?

I'm sitting in my wheelchair now,
Watching the world go by,
People stop to look and stare,
As if I am just not even there,
I know I am different, I know I am,
But why can't they see me for who I really am?
I may not be able to walk again,
But why can't I just be the same as them?
I have a helper at my school,
She takes me out of lesson to the main hall,
The wheels are my legs,
You don't know how it feels,
To know it just won't heal,
But things can be good being disabled,
It's not all bad, it's really not,
I've been through quite a lot,
You have to admire,
My strengths and desires,
To get on in the world
And live my life!
So next time you see someone just like me,
Think to yourself, who would you rather be,
Someone like you, or someone disabled like me?

Stephanie Randleson (13)
Sanders Draper School

What It Would Be Like To Be A Footballer

Scoring on TV on the pitch,
You wouldn't have any trouble, you'd be dirty rich,
Playing for a high class team,
When you come on the pitch, the fans' faces will beam,
If you could handle this,
Then *hip hip hooray* you could be a footballer one day.

Darryl Wyatt (11)
Sanders Draper School

I Wonder What It Is Like To Be . . .

I wonder what it is like to be,
A story that never ends?
Give them to people on their birthday
Which people always send.

I wonder what it would be like to be a pencil
Doing people's work?
When the teacher comes,
She's marking good homework.

What would it be like, I wonder,
To be the Crown Jewels?
Everyone admiring my gold,
Surely that's my wish?

I wonder what it is like to be,
A ruler measuring everything?
I would be proud
Of my name (the measuring thing).

I wish I was an aeroplane,
Flying very high,
Really high, really high,
In the big, blue sky.

Edward Douglas Melrose (11)
Sanders Draper School

What's It Like To Be?

What's it like to be a footballer?
Scoring goals on and off the pitch,
Doing it all day and ending up rich,
Buying mansions here and there,
Well, you're rich, why should you care?
Beating your rivals, getting it over and done
And beating the champions, 3 goals to 1,
Having loads of fans, south, east and west,
We all know being a football player is certainly the best!

Jack Sullivan (11)
Sanders Draper School

I Wonder What It Would Be Like . . .

I wonder what it is like to be a plane,
Soaring above the sky,
Flying through the clouds,
Being able to fly?

I wonder what it is like to be a CD,
Spinning round and round?
Speakers turned all the way up,
Making lots of sound.

I wonder what it is like to be a hat,
Sitting on someone's head,
Not doing anything all day,
Wishing I was dead?

I wonder what it is like to be a whale,
Eating all day,
Stuffing my face with plankton,
Like an open sea buffet?

Michael Chaplin (13)
Sanders Draper School

I Wonder What It's Like To Be A Ghost?

I wonder what it's like to be a ghost,
Running around, running through posts,
Going around, giving people heart attacks,
Creeping up behind their backs?

I wonder if ghosts play football,
Or go to parties in a big hall?
I wonder if ghosts dream at night,
Or have nightmares and give themselves a fright?

I wonder, if I was a ghost,
Would I run around, running through posts?
Would I go around giving people heart attacks
And creep up behind their backs?

Tom Pockett (13)
Sanders Draper School

I Wonder What It Would Be Like To Be A . . .

I wonder what it would be like to be a butterfly,
To fly softly through the pretty blue sky,
Where would I go,
What would I know?

I wonder what it would be like to be a horse?
Riding through the wood with a force,
The clip-clopping of my hooves,
My owner telling me to move.

I wonder what it would be like to be a dolphin,
To glide through the sea using my fins?
I could go anywhere I wished
And go swimming with the other fish.

I wonder what it would be like to be a bird?
I could talk to my friends with twittering words,
I would make my nest,
From only the best.

I wonder what it would be like to be a ghost,
Not being able to touch even a post?
Would my family and friends be able to see me?
I could go to the cinema,
Without paying the entrance fee.

Or would I prefer just being me?

Rebecca Hawkins (13)
Sanders Draper School

What Is It Like?

What is it like to live on the street
With nothing to eat and nothing on your feet?
Sitting on the street, wondering where I am going to sleep,
One day I wish to have lots to eat and something on my feet,
Knowing where I am going to sleep.

Lloyd Anderson (13)
Sanders Draper School

I Wonder What It's Like To Be An Eye?

I wonder what it's like to be an eye,
Blinking once again,
Staring out to the open world,
Exploding under the watery strain?

This is when I shed a tear,
Now I can't see out at all,
I'm so full up with water,
I think I'm going to fall.

Every day I see something new,
I wonder what they are,
I cannot think, I can only see,
But I'm doing well so far.

It's the end of the day,
It's time to have a rest,
I close my eyes tightly,
I know I've tried my best.

Nadene Kennedy (13)
Sanders Draper School

What Is It Like To Be . . . A Tramp?

What is it like to be a tramp
Living in the damp, cold street?
What is it like when no one cares
When walking past, people look at their feet?

How does it feel to be all alone
Your home changing from week to week?
You want to have millions of pounds by your name
But sadly, pennies are all you can seek.

When was the last time you felt safe and warm
Is what I would like to know?
Feeling scared when experiencing a storm
How would you feel if you experienced this woe?

Faye McInerney (14)
Sanders Draper School

What It Is Like To Be A Hostage

Day after day I sit and wait,
Will they let me go or will I have to stay?
There's nothing else to do, than to think of the worst,
What must my family be feeling?

Tears run down my face,
I try to be brave,
But I just can't stop thinking,
What will they do next?

It's a dream, it's got to be,
I've been here three weeks now,
I just wish I would wake up.

Why is this happening to me?
All I can do is sit and wait,
Will they let me go,
Or will I have to stay?

Victoria Coleman (13)
Sanders Draper School

What Is It Like To Be Abused?

What is it like to be abused?
Battered, beaten, bleeding and bruised.
What is it like to be scared in your own home
Worried that you will end up alone?

What is it like to be thinking of taking your own life?
Just you, alone, in the kitchen, with a knife . . .
What is it like to be afraid to tell a soul
No one to turn to, no one to hold?

What is it like to be scared of going out
To be frightened of what people will ask about?
Wanting to fly away, be as free as a dove,
But you won't, you are sticking around, for love.

Hayley Stubbington (13)
Sanders Draper School

I Wonder What It Would Be Like . . .

I wonder what it would be like,
To be a trillionaire,
Buying lots of expensive gifts,
Such as a golden chair?

I wonder what it would be like,
To be a golf ball,
Being hit by a golf club
And landing in the city hall?

I wonder what it would be like,
To be a monkey,
Going to the monkey dance?
Boy, I hope it's funky!

I wonder what it would be like,
To be a juicy mango,
Being squished into a blender,
Then poured into a can on Tango?

I wonder what it would be like,
To be a tall tree,
Gazing at the moonlight,
While people pee on me?

Constantinos Panayi (11)
Sanders Draper School

What Is It Like To Be?

What is it like to be a child on the streets,
Sleeping in bins, with little to eat?
What is it like to have no friends,
To know that tomorrow might be your end?
What is it like to be freezing cold,
Knowing you may be until you're very old?
What is it like to have no family?
They're in a warm house like you're supposed to be.
Starving, freezing, homeless, alone,
Awaiting, dreading the end.

Sean Wade (12)
Sanders Draper School

I Wonder What It's Like To Be . . .

I wonder what it's like to be,
A leaf hanging from a tree,
Where and which way will the wind take me?

I wonder what it's like to be,
My mum looking after me,
Cooking, cleaning, washing and ironing
And still smiling with glee?

I wonder what it's like to be,
My friend for a day,
Thinking what she thinks,
Listening to what she has to say?

I wonder what it's like to be,
A black and yellow honeybee,
Flitting around for hours a day,
Making honey for my tea?

I wonder what it's like to be,
A dancer performing on a stage,
Around a chair, on the stairs,
Or even locked in a cage?

Laura Pickess (13)
Sanders Draper School

I Wonder What It Is Like To Be A Woman?

I wonder what it is like to be a woman,
Always doing the chores?
That includes doing the floors.

I wonder what it is like to be a camera,
Always taking photos
And putting on slide shows?

I wonder what it would be like to be a football,
Always being kicked around
And then feeling great
When I am found?

Billy Miller (11)
Sanders Draper School

I Wonder What It's Like To Be . . .

I wonder what it's like to be,
A monkey swinging on a tree,
Eating bananas and waiting to be set free?

I wonder what it's like to be,
A baby sitting on her grandad's knee?
Thirteen years ago, that was me.

I wonder what it's like to be,
Thierry Henry scoring goals and keeping fit?
Playing for Arsenal and France, he's always a hit.

I wonder what it's like to be,
A soldier out in Iraq,
Fighting for peace and carrying a gun on your back?

I wonder what it's like to be,
Out at sea with the waves crashing
And the sun burning down on me?

I wonder what it's like to be,
The sun, so far away,
Being loved by everyone?

I wonder what it's like to be,
A celebrity, swanning around,
Saying, 'Take a photo of me.'

Sarah Bonnici (13)
Sanders Draper School

My Mate, Sunny

My mate Sunny
Had no money
He has a baby bunny
He's got a big tummy
And his food is yummy
That is why
He's got a big tummy.

Reece Spencer (12)
Sanders Draper School

I Wonder What It's Like To Be . . .

I wonder what it's like to be
Prime Minister of the UK
Working night and day?

I wonder what it's like to be
A teacher in a school
Where pupils break the rules?

I wonder what it's like to be
An elephant in a zoo
With nothing much to do?

I wonder what it's like to be
A dog without a home
Always free to roam?

I wonder what it's like to be
A prisoner on Death Row
Wondering when you'll go?

I wonder what it's like to be
A poor, young boy
Who hasn't any toys?

Adam Oxley (13)
Sanders Draper School

What Is It Like To Be?

What is it like to be a child on the streets?
Sleeping in bins with little to eat,
What is it like to have no friends?
To know that tomorrow might bring your end,
What is it like to be freezing cold?
Knowing you may be until you're very old,
What is it like to have no family?
They're in the warm house like you're supposed to be,
Starving, freezing, homeless, alone,
Awaiting, dreading the end.

Neil Moran (12)
Sanders Draper School

War

The war is over
But people are still dying
They are taking prisoners
People crying.

We thought they had given up
But obviously not
They have put the killings on the net
They have killed a lot.

People's weeping families
Crying a lot
They never saw it coming
Him getting shot.

Hopefully the war is now over
America helped us loads
If they do not give up
Their town will explode.

Michael Ireland (13)
Sanders Draper School

What Is It Like To Be A . . .

What is it like to be a hostage?
To be imprisoned for no crime
To know you will be dead in a short time
And to be used as a tool.

What is it like to be a hostage?
To be threatened for your life
To think you will not see your husband or wife
And to be alone.

What is it like to be a hostage?
To run from your gloom
To be caught and beaten, then face your doom
And is that what it's like to be a hostage?

Ian Hayfield (12)
Sanders Draper School

I Wonder What It's Like To Be A Celebrity

I wonder what it's like to be
A huge, sexy celebrity
With long blonde hair and teeth that shine?
That is the dream of mine.

I wonder what it's like to be
Living in a huge house by the sea
Wearing all my expensive jewellery?

I wonder what it's like to be
Living in another country
Swimming with the fishes all around the sea?

I wonder what it's like to be
Making lots of money
Singing things that sound funny?

I wonder what it's like to be
Singing on TV with a celebrity that hates me?
I wonder what it's like to be
Having people look at me whilst I'm on TV?

I wonder what it's like
Just being *me!*

Samantha Jenkins (14)
Sanders Draper School

What Is It Like To Be Abused?

Scared and alone, left for dead
Blood trickling down my head.
Nowhere to run to, nowhere to go,
Who do I tell? I don't know.
I've been abused, not been fed,
Got messy hair, got no bed.
So now I know how it feels,
To have a scar that never heals.
I think I know now, I can bet,
That I am just an unwanted pet.

Rose Pettit (12)
Sanders Draper School

What Is It Like To Be A Tramp?

What is it like to be a tramp
Lying in a cardboard box,
Huddled in the corner streets,
Crumpled on the cold, dark rocks?

Talkative people pass by and stare,
They stroll along without a thought,
Of what it would be like to be,
A tramp of any sort.

Food is nowhere to be found,
When you're a tramp with nothing,
Crumbs are a rich meal,
To a tramp who's always running.

Their palace is a dumpster
And their gowns are rags and cloth,
A cold is a deadly disease,
Your death, to which you cough.

Jessica Saville (13)
Sanders Draper School

What Is It Like To Be In A Fire?

What is it like to be in a fire
Trapped with no way out,
Cowering in a corner
With no one to hear you shout?

Your skin blistering and burning,
Coughing, suffocating, begging to choke,
If the flames don't get you,
You'll be caught by the smoke.

You can't run, you can't hide,
You can't escape to the other side,
All the things you wish you'd said,
But now it's too late, because you're dead.

Terry Bradbrook (13)
Sanders Draper School

Thoughts . . .

What is it like to be in the Third World,
With hunger, pain and dehydration?
People scared, people unhappy and worst of all, it was the smell.
What is it like to be?

What is it like to be in Iraq?
Pitiful children, adults and families,
Whilst all the fighting is in the dark,
What is it like to be?

What is it like to be in a flood,
With people around you drowning, drowning?
The town is ruined, with drained-out mud,
What is it like to be?

These thoughts just run through my head,
I think of this all the time.
What would it be like,
In one of these situations?

Nicky Wells (13)
Sanders Draper School

I Wonder What It Is Like To Be An Angel?

I wonder what it is like to be a dolphin,
Who swims all day in the shining sea?

I wonder what it is like to be an angel,
Who is up in Heaven all day and comes out to fly at night?

I wonder what it is like to be a sparkling, yellow star,
That's high in the sky and shines down on everyone?

I wonder what it is like to be a butterfly,
Who has beautiful colours on its wings?

I wonder what it is like to be fireworks,
That have beautiful patterns and colours and makes people smile?

Marianna Alexandrou (13)
Sanders Draper School

I Wonder What It Is Like To Be . . .

I wonder what it is like to be
A cat sleeping on a bed,
Then standing in the kitchen
Waiting to be fed?

I wonder what it is like to be
A door standing in a house,
With a little hole in it
Made by a mouse?

I wonder what it is like to be
A wall standing in a street,
Always being kicked
By little children's feet?

I wonder what it is like to be
A star always in the sky?
Twinkle, shine, twinkle, shine
I am very high.

I wonder what it is like to be
A snail moving very slow?
It would take a whole day
Just to get back home.

Ashleigh Couchman (11)
Sanders Draper School

What's It Like To Be . . .

What's it like to be chewing gum,
Under the table, day by day,
Getting harder and harder.

What's it like to be a chair,
Getting sat on by different bums,
Sweaty ones, skinny ones, fat ones, firm ones.

What's it like to be the sun,
Sending heat to everyone,
Making sure that they have fun.

Gabriel Adedipe (11)
Sanders Draper School

What It Would Be Like If . . .

What it would be like if I was homeless . . .

Out in the cold on a winter's night
Out in the blazing sun
No one there to care for me
No home, no food, no one.

What it would be like if I was homeless . . .

Sleeping on cardboard
Looking in bins
Asking for money
No one there to care for me.

What it would be like if I was homeless . . .

One pair of shoes all year
People looking at you as they walk by
No one there to care for me.

Lauren Connelly (11)
Sanders Draper School

What's It Like To Be A Terrorist?

I feel that it's my duty,
That I will be rewarded,
If I do this,
I will be honoured.

I sacrifice the lives of others,
Not forgetting my own,
I ignore the pleads to make me stop
And I deafen out the cries and screams.

What's it like to be a terrorist?
I have no life,
So what's the point of living?
With my death,
I send pain and suffering to the world . . .

John Wilson (13)
Sanders Draper School

I Wonder What It Would Be Like

What would it be like
To be an ocean
Crashing against the sand?

What would it be like
To have the power
To smother the land?

Would I make gentle noises
While someone became tanned?

Or would I miss the feeling
Of holding someone's hand?

Would I treasure the creatures
That caress my waves?

Or would I miss the long walks
Within my jagged caves?

Would I miss the views
As far as the eye can see?

Or would I miss just being me?

Jamie Keddy (13)
Sanders Draper School

What Is It Like To Be?

What is it like to be a ball
So round and small
Rolling around and around the school hall?

What is it like to be a rat
Scurrying around the dirty, old flat
Trying to avoid the black and white cat?

What is it like to be a shower
Getting switched on and off, hour upon hour
To get people smelling like a flower?

Samuel Watson (11)
Sanders Draper School

I Wonder What It Is Like To Be . . .

I wonder what it is like to be an astronaut,
Having no matter outside of your suit.

I wonder what it is like to be a cell,
Being the smallest, living thing on Earth.

I wonder what it is like to be a book,
With all those words people read.

I wonder what it is like to be a soldier,
Shooting and running and fighting in every war.

I wonder what it is like to be a fish,
Looking at those beautiful oceans and having to breathe in water.

I wonder what it is like to be a teacher,
Telling naughty students to work.

I wonder what it is like to be a nuclear atom,
Seeing all those years go by.

I wonder what it is like to be so many things,
That are impossible to be.

Sebastian Massart (13)
Sanders Draper School

What's It Like To Be . . .

What's it like to be a parrot,
Gliding through the summer sky?

Red, blue, green and yellow,
Black eyes, watching from afar.

Through the trees, he swiftly goes,
Searching for a tasty treat.

Handsome and proud, he stands alone,
Feathers bright and clean.

The call of the others beckon him
And off he goes again.

Siân Roberts (11)
Sanders Draper School

All The Wonders

I wonder what it's like to be floating through the sky,
Upon the clouds and past the birds,
Free from all that pry?

I wonder what it would be like to be an angel up above,
Free from troubles down below,
Living happily, full of love?

I wonder what it would be like to be a blanket of fallen snow,
Here one day and gone the next,
Why do I have to go?

I wonder what it would be like to be a star up in the sky,
Shining brightly for all to see,
When the night is nigh?

I wonder what it would be like to be a shell amongst the sand,
Taken home by little children,
All across the land?

I wonder what it would be like to be someone you never could,
Changing who you truly were?
I don't think I ever would.

Katie Markham   (13)
Sanders Draper School

What Is It Like To Be . . .

What is it like to be a footballer,
To wear designer gear with coats of fur?

What is it like to be a tramp,
To be miserable and live in the damp?

What is it like to be a bird,
To fly the skies and not speak a word?

What is it like to be a fish?
To be able to breathe underwater is everyone's wish.

What is it like to be a sweet,
To be adored and chosen over meat?

George James Hills   (11)
Sanders Draper School

I Wonder What It's Like To Be . . .

I wonder what it's like to be . . .
A fish, a key, a trampoline?
Big and black, white and bright
I'd like to be
A starry night.

I wonder what it's like to be . . .
A table, a tree, a symphony?
Jumping high with all my might
I'd like to be
A flying kite.

I wonder what it's like to be . . .
A plug, a lion, a tangerine?
Stretchy and thin, dark or light
I'd like to be
A pair of tights.

I wonder what it's like to be . . .
A shoe, a plum, a drummer's drum?
Green and spiky, makes you glee
I'd like to be
A Christmas tree.

Francesca Harper (13)
Sanders Draper School

What Is It Like To Be Wayne Rooney?

What is it like to be Wayne Rooney,
To drive the fans loony?
What is it like to come out your door?
What is it like to get taken to the floor?

What is it like to drive a nice car?
In his career, he will go far.
What is it like to have loads of money?
What is it like to live somewhere sunny?

Matthew Peacock (13)
Sanders Draper School

I Wonder What It's Like To Be

I wonder what it's like to be
A fly on the wall,
If you could really earwig
And spy on them all.

I wonder what it's like to be
A punchbag getting battered,
If you got punched so much
And if it really mattered.

I wonder what it's like to be
A world famous movie star,
Drinking champagne
In a chauffeur driven car.

I wonder what it's like to be
A bird flying high,
To everybody else
Being a speck in the sky.

Daniel Hooper (13)
Sanders Draper School

What It Would Be Like If I Was Famous

What it would be like if I was famous,
Making sure I look okay,
People wanting to get my autograph,
Doing something different every day?

Seeing my face on the front of magazines and papers,
Sometimes looking good, sometimes bad,
Rushing around from each interview and photo shoot,
But people who don't like me, they make me sad.

I miss my family and friends
And having my own privacy,
I think I would prefer to be normal
And relaxed and not always so busy.

Catherine Hutchinson (12)
Sanders Draper School

I Wonder What It's Like To Be . . .

I wonder what it's like to be
A soldier signed up for the army
Leaving home and saying goodbyes
Eating a family meal of salami?

I wonder what it's like to be
A soldier in and out the war?
Seeing people die in battle
Death rates going up more and more.

I wonder what it's like to be
A soldier with a hi-tech gun
Face to face to the enemy
Have to kill but cannot run?

I wonder what it's like to be
A soldier not knowing what will happen?
Maybe victory or maybe not
Just hope the war will end right now.

I wonder what it's like to be
A soldier to die as a brave hero?
Bang!
Died knowing, that is how it ends
Now taking a trip down memory lane.

Lisa Chong (13)
Sanders Draper School

What Is It Like To Be A Homeless Child?

What is it like to be a homeless child?
Do they get hungry and lost in the wild?
Do they search for scraps and mouldy food?
Are they starving? They're not in the mood.

With no one to love them and no one to care,
They never wash or brush their hair,
They are very bored and have no fun
And no one to hug, they have no mum!

Zac Chouman (13)
Sanders Draper School

I Wonder What It Is Like To Be . . .

I wonder what it is like to be
An eagle flying all day
Sweeping down with my sharp claws
To catch my fleeing prey?

I wonder what it is like to be
A person living in Iraq
With no food and war all around them
It would be too much pressure on my back?

I wonder what it is like to be
A computer with so much knowledge?
Because I would be smart enough
I wouldn't have to go to college.

I wonder what it is like to be
A famous football star
Earning big bucks an hour?
I'd be able to afford caviar.

I wonder what it is like to be
The almighty and powerful God
The one who has the power over all human life?
And I bet he likes cod!

Scott Jenkins (13)
Sanders Draper School

I Wonder What It's Like To Be A . . .

I wonder what it's like to be a shark,
Way down in the deep?
To be honest, there's not a lot to eat.

I wonder what it's like to be a cat?
Always landing on my feet and meeting other cats,
But watch out for the freaks.

I wonder what it's like to be a dog?
Always barking, eating one type of food.

Tom Wood
Sanders Draper School

I Wonder What It Is Like To Be . . .

What is it like to be a young runaway?
To be on the run, all of the day
Nobody likes him, not even his mum
Or that's what he thought
And that's why he's dumb
He has lots of problems that won't go away
So he thinks wildly about them all through the day
His dad blamed him for everything
Even his own departure
He said that he hated his son
Just because he was disabled
His dad was a rancid man, one full of depression
Thanks to his awful dad, he was on this mission
On cold days when all was bad
A tear rolled down his cheek
He never found the love he longed to seek
He hated living all over the place
For he was a no-hope case
Now his life was set in stone
And he was forever on his own.

Alfie Sears (12)
Sanders Draper School

What Is It Like?

What is it like to be a child on the street
With no education and nothing to eat?
Walking around, not knowing where to sleep.
Then being followed by some old creep.
City yobs throw cans at you,
But yet they don't know what you're going through.
Another night sleeping in a cold shop door.
Wonder if anyone else is this poor?
So next time you see a child on the street,
Don't walk on by,
Stop and throw some change by their feet.

Emma Matthews (13)
Sanders Draper School

What Would It Be Like If My Mum Went Away?

I don't know where you are, Mum,
I hope you are okay,
I have been thinking of you all day,
I hope you are thinking of me too,
Wherever you are, I really miss you.

I don't know where you are, Mum,
I hope you are okay,
We are all so worried, Mum,
You've been gone since May,
Please Mum, hurry and come home,
Since you've been gone, I've been so alone.

I don't know where you are, Mum,
I hope you are okay,
But just in case you don't return,
I have something to say:

Thank you for the great love you gave me.
I love you so much, hope you love me.

Jade Rogers (12)
Sanders Draper School

I Wonder What It's Like To Be?

I wonder what it's like to be a cat,
To climb trees and jump in the air?

I wonder what it's like to be a dog,
Guard my house and wag my wonderful tail?

I wonder what it's like to be a bird,
Soaring through the wind and be like an angel in the air?

I wonder what it's like to be a snake
And not chew my food and slide on the ground?

I wonder what it's like to be a shark
And have over 100 teeth and have fins?

Tom Yems (13)
Sanders Draper School

I Wonder

I wonder what it's like
To be a star
To be high in the sky
Away so far . . . ?

I wonder what it's like
To be an eye,
To be able to see things high up
Towards the sky,
Or to see something that makes you cry?
That's what I think it's like to be an eye . . .

I wonder what it's like
To be a horse
To gallop around that hard jumping course,
To have a heavy saddle on my back
Then to be kicked right in the rib rack . . . ?

I wonder what it's like
To be the heart
To be the most important body part
To pump and pump all day long
And if I should stop, it would be wrong . . .

I wonder what it's like
To be a ghost?
They're the ones who have fun the most
To wander around while no one can see me
To scare people is so easy . . .

I wonder what it's like
To be the brain
To think all day long until I go insane
To be the quickest brain of them all
To be quick, sharp and on the ball?

Lauren Feeney (13)
Sanders Draper School

My Pet, Bassy

I have a pet called Bassy
She is a tri-coloured Bassett
Plodding around the garden and house
With her chunky paws
She likes a bit of football and tug-of-war
Not even tiring
'Where does she get her energy?' we all say
Everyone thinks she's cute and cuddly.

But she has an angry side
Barking and growling
Whenever she's annoyed
She likes to bite anything in sight
Even human skin
So don't run away
Or she'll chase you with her gnashing teeth.

Graham Carter (11)
Sanders Draper School

September 11th

Can you remember,
The 11th of September,
When there was no peace, only war?
That was not what we were looking for.

Bin Laden's crew,
Hijacked out of the blue
And sad times hit the USA,
Because of Bin Laden's cruel ways.

Many died,
Few survived,
So please stop to remember,
The 11th of September.

Tom Bonnett (12)
Sanders Draper School

My Dad Is . . .

My dad is so fat
He has a black and white cat
That stands on the wall
And likes to call
Miaow, miaow!
My dad shouts, *'Yeow!'*
Cos she bites my dad's bum.

My dad is so hairy
He looks like our canary
Which sits on the top of the cage
He looks a bit beige
He likes to chirp
My dad likes to burp
And they're both as noisy as each other.

Kelsey Bond (11)
Sanders Draper School

If I Were A Teacher . . .

If I were a teacher . . .
I'd ditch the uniform
I'd change the school dinners
To some sweets or popcorn.

If I were a teacher . . .
I'd give more days off school
I'd let there be more playtime
And some lessons in the pool.

If I were a teacher . . .
I wouldn't get the sack
The kids would cause a riot
Because they'd want me back!

Jack Greener (11)
Sanders Draper School

Abused

What it is like to be a child who gets abused?
Nowhere
To get help and to be cared for
Confused
So cold and hurt, he is covered in
Horrible, black dirt
Evil
His parents, so cold-hearted,
Where is the love that they can bring to this boy
That has been ripped apart?
Always
He will have that picture in his head
Of him, in the gutter, abused and dead!
Never
Will he forget what people can do
So ask yourself this question,
'What if I were that child?'
Because it could be you!

Jennifer Gammans (13)
Sanders Draper School

Seasons

Autumn time is here
The dusk is coming fast
Winter's round the corner
The snow on the grass.

Christmas time is pending
Presents below the trees
Spring has sprung again
Flowers to please me.

Summer sunshine so bright
Evenings are so light
Autumn comes around again
Oh, those dark nights!

Taylor Nathaniel (12)
Sanders Draper School

What Would It Be Like To Be A Rat?

What would it be like to be a rat
Trying to keep out of the way of the cat?
Scurrying away from the kitty,
Through the drains of the city.

Being able to shrink,
Means that I can run up the sink,
Oh to get away from the cat,
Please turn me into a bat.

What would it be like to be a bat
To fly around at night,
Looking for something to bite?
You can reach great heights,
Flying as high as kites.

Sleeping upside down all day,
Hiding out of the way,
Until I feel the moon,
That's when I start my reign of doom.

Jonathan Golder (11)
Sanders Draper School

Splat Cat

One day I saw a cat
A big, scary, black cat
It followed me home, until I crossed the road
Behind me I heard the rumble of a heavy load.

After that, the cat never followed me home
I felt so alone . . .
I heard truckers talking of disgusting things
About the animals in front of their steering screens
Before they disappeared under their trucks
Now I know what happened, perhaps that cat
Had not had such good luck.

James O'Vens (11)
Sanders Draper School

Alone

I wonder what it's like to be . . .

What is it like to be with nobody else?
Sitting there, crying there, homelessness
I cry every day, wishing I was there,
Wishing I was very warm and really under care.

I have no one else and I am on my own,
Nothing to eat but a pale, cold bone.
I wish I had a cuddle and a nice, loving home,
I wish I was happy and not on my own.

Please think about me and think how I feel,
Wish I had a family and a proper meal.
I wish I went to school and learnt something,
I wonder, I wonder, if I'd get anything?

Yarlinie Thana (12)
Sanders Draper School

Magic

Magic, what is magic?
Wizards, witches and black cats?
Fluffy white bunnies popping out of black hats?
Swirls of glitter, spirals of dust,
Strange, purple winds that pass in a gust?

Magic, what is it?
People who vanish, gone in mid-air?
Bare-handed men who wrestle with bears?
Genies big and tied in a knot,
Appearing mysteriously from a golden teapot?

This is magic!
Magic is fairies, goblins and elves,
Night-time nymphs who dance by themselves,
Eyes staring from under the stones,
Hideous gargoyles and wrinkled-up gnomes.

Mia Morlang (11)
Sanders Draper School

What Is It Like To Be An Abused Child?

What is it like to be an abused child?
How would you feel, not wanted and alone?
How would you feel, day after day, beaten and bullied?
What would you feel like?

Sitting there, calling for help and nobody comes,
Laying there, with visions of hitting and beating running
                                        through your mind,
Not sure what's next or what to expect,
What would you do?

Your family not wanting you, isolating you every day,
All you want is to fit in, to be loved and cared for,
Wanting to be hugged and kissed goodnight, but it's all dreams,
What would you feel like?

Fell over and hurt yourself, hoping someone will come and hug you,
Ending up in tears and pain,
Ending up in suicide and torture to yourself,
What would you do?

Abusing a child, making them feel cold and scared,
You're heartless, selfish, sick and evil,
If you were that child,
What would you feel like?

They lay there, sleepless nights,
Dreaming of love, care, joyfulness,
Why not give them that instead of a beating and a punch?
I don't understand why you don't use them for your love,
                                        not a punchbag?

What is it like to be an abused child?
How would you feel, not wanted and alone?
How would you feel, day after day, beaten and bullied?
What would you feel like?

Megan Knowler (12)
Sanders Draper School

Homelessness

What is it like to be a young child scrapping in the streets.
Never knowing when your next meal is going to come.
When you sit on the side of the road,
When it's raining or even snowing.
But inside, you heart is still glowing.

When you are sitting on the roadside,
Begging for money from strangers.
Sitting alone, wondering when you will next see someone you know,
But other than that, feeling quite low.

And you are thinking about where your family are
And if they are searching through rubbish bins for food,
Just like you.

As people walk past they point and stare,
Looking at your unbrushed hair.

But one day, someone comes and sits beside you and says,
'I can take you to a shelter,
Where you can become much healthier.'

In the shelter, all the people are the same as you,
But then you catch someone's eye, you become all shy,
The lady begins to cry,
It's your mother,
She hugs and kisses you.
You move into your own house,
You go to school
And your mother has a job.
You now have a new life.

Jessica Negus (12)
Sanders Draper School

What Is It Like To Be A Homeless Person?

What is it like to be a homeless person?
Laying in the streets,
With nothing to put on your feet.

What is it like to be a homeless person?
When it grows dark and time to sleep,
All you have to keep you warm,
Is a blanket which barely touches your toes.

What is it like to be a homeless person?
That has to beg to make a living,
When people come along and kick you,
They think you are just a piece of rubbish.

What is it like to be a homeless person?
With no food in your stomach,
Trying to find scraps to calm the hunger,
Until the soup trolley comes,
To get some food in your body.

What is it like to be a homeless person?
'I'm free, I'm free,
No bills to pay,
I'm free!'

Jack McLellan (12)
Sanders Draper School

What Is It Like To Be Homeless?

What is it like to be homeless?
Living on the street,
With nothing much to eat.

What is it like to be homeless?
With people staring at you,
There is nothing they can do.

What is it like to be homeless?
Sleeping on street corners,
With nothing to order.

What is it like to be homeless?
With no money,
It isn't funny.

What is it like to be homeless?
Searching through bins,
Looking in every tin.

What is it like to be homeless?
Living on the street,
With nothing much to eat.

Joe Webster (13)
Sanders Draper School

What Is It Like To Be . . .

What is it like to be a soldier in Iraq,
With the evil, mad terrorists?
You will have to watch your back,
Putting your life on the line
For stupid politicians,
There was a massive protest,
But of course, they didn't listen.

The evil scum, Bin Laden and his terrorist organisation,
Bring death, fear and sorrow for hundreds of countries and nations,
The war was meant to find weapons which could kill many,
It's gone on for a year and so far, we ain't found any!

Daniel Snow (12)
Sanders Draper School

What Is It Like To Be A Teacher's Pest?

What is it like to be a teacher's pest?
Getting told off, putting those horrid teachers to the test.
Getting shouted at without fail,
Until they make the teachers wail.

Don't do your work all the time,
Bully people, think it's fine, work can never be as neat as mine.
Shouting curses across the classroom,
Never stop doing it till after noon.

When you go home, teachers breathe a sigh of relief,
For it was that person who was a naughty chief.
The teacher clears up all your rubble,
Knowing tomorrow will be another day of . . .

Trouble!

Peter Otuwehinmi (11)
Sanders Draper School

What Is It Like To Be A Child In The Beslan Siege?

What is it like to be a child in the Beslan siege?
What does it feel like to be terrified at school?
Where you feel the most secure,
What would you do?

What does it feel like not knowing when you're going to eat again?
What does it feel like, thinking you might die?
If you were there,
What would you do?

What does it feel like to watch your own friends die,
To know you're never going to see them again?
If that was you,
What would you do?

Rebecca Warren (13)
Sanders Draper School

I Wonder What It Is Like To Be?

I wonder what it is like to be
Sick, hungry and tired.

Going to school, so happy with glee
Wondering what friends I might see.

In the playground
Saying goodbye to Mum, Dad and Gran.

When inside men run in holding guns
Bombs on their belts
I wanted to shout, 'Help, help, help!'

Starved and scared
Longing for Mum
I thought I might die
I just felt numb.

A bomb went off, the roof caved in
What the hell happened to President Poutin?

We all got up and ran
Bullets whizzed past
Friends fell down like flies
But I just prayed
And ran, ran, ran.

Christopher Beckwith (13)
Sanders Draper School

What Is It Like To Be . . .

What is it like to be an Iraqi citizen?
What is it like to wake up to the sound of bombs and gunfire?
What is it like to be separated from your family
Or forced to fight because you can lift a gun and operate it?
What is it like to fear for your life
Because of someone else's quarrel?
What is it like to walk down a street
Where on both sides, there are armed soldiers
Who even in your own country, look at you like an outcast?
What is it like to look out of a window at a soldier
And wonder if they even care the slightest bit about you?
Do they have a soul at all?
What is it like to think that one day it could be over,
One day the armies could be gone,
The wounds could be healed
And you could carry on where you left off?
But what would it be like to know
That there will always be a wound that will never heal,
A scar for life, not just on you, but on your whole country?
People have lost lives, family and hope.
The armies will leave, but the sadness, the anger
And the disgrace will never leave any of you.

Ryan Havis (12)
Sanders Draper School

What Is It Like To Be?

I wonder what it is like to be a tiger,
Lurching through the grass all day?
I wonder what it is like to be a tiger?

I wonder what it would be like to be homeless,
Living on the streets?
I wonder what it would be like to be homeless,
No home, no bed, nothing to eat?

I wonder what it would be like to be the floor,
To be trod on every day?
I wonder what it would be like to be the floor,
Leaving marks that won't go away?

I wonder what it would be like to be a dog,
Going for walks every day?
I wonder what it would be like to be a dog,
Scaring cats and making them go away?

Holly Louise Griffin (11)
Sanders Draper School

What Is It Like To Be A Teacher?

Here I go again, getting up early
To go on my long journey.
Moaning teachers in the staffroom,
Nagging about kids.
Ah, silence in the classroom.
Bell rings, kids come in shouting and screaming,
Kids yelling, 'Miss, Miss,' my head is going to burst.
I can't get any peace.
I feel like sticking my head in a tank of piranhas.
I can't take it any more, *'Quiet!'* I shout.
The class is silent.
They start talking again.
Here the long journey starts once again.

Chereena Harriott (11)
Sanders Draper School

What Is It Like To Be . . .

What is it like to be a teacher?
Shouting and talking to children all day.

What is it like to be a teacher?
Drinking coffee and gossiping
In the staffroom at lunch and break.

What is it like to be a teacher?
Sitting in bed, marking students' work.

What is it like to be a teacher?
Helping children do their work.

What is it like to be a teacher?
Enjoying long holidays.

What is it like to be a teacher?
Perhaps I will find out one day.

Ellë Mortimer (11)
Sanders Draper School

What's It Like To Be?

What's it like to be a fish,
Swimming around, until dead on a dish?

What's it like to be a cat,
Sleeping all day, on the doormat?

What's it like to be the sun,
Shining all day, letting everyone have fun?

What's it like to be a light,
On for hours, shining bright?

What's it like to be a tree,
Standing tall for all to see?

What's it like to be a telephone,
Ringing non-stop for all to moan?

Claire Caston (12)
Sanders Draper School

What's It Like To Be . . .

What's it like to be a dog?
Sometimes smelly,
Bit like a hog!

What's it like to be a cat?
People patting you,
Pat, pat, pat!

What's it like to be a bird?
Singing in the morning,
Just to be heard!

What's it like to be a fish?
Staying clear
Of a silver food dish!

What's it like to be one of me?
Wait until you become one,
But until then,
Look in the mirror
And you will see!

Susan Weatherley (11)
Sanders Draper School

I Wonder What It Is Like To Be?

I wonder what it is like to be a rabbit,
Eating a carrot and playing with my family?

I wonder what it is like to be a fish,
Swimming around in the sea?

I wonder what it is like to be a dog,
Living with my family and having a cuddle?

I wonder what it is like to be a cat,
Saying a *miaow* and licking my paws?

I wonder what it is like to be a horse,
Running around the field and eating food?

Vanisha Patel (12)
Sanders Draper School

What Is It Like To Be A Monkey?

What is it like to be a monkey?
Swinging from tree to tree
Up in the jungle
Where my monkey friends are with me.

Eating and chilling
Is what we do best.

Munching bananas, picking our fleas
I'm all for it, as long as they're leading the way.

Our mums and dads
Are looking after the young ones
Whilst we play
Trying not to wake the rest.

Dominique Dyett (11)
Sanders Draper School

What Is It Like To Be?

What is it like to be in a fire?
All you can see is ferocious flames,
People screaming, people shouting,
Smelling the burning, brings you to tears.

The crumbling of the building,
The constant smoke,
You can just imagine the blistering and burning
And the heat and gas which is given off.

The screaming people getting buried,
The fire engine putting it out,
Gallons of water going on, saving innocent lives
And all to no avail, their lives taken.

What is it like to be a relative,
Whose mum and dad have just been killed,
Or being the one with no more life,
Living in darkness now?

Jamie Taylor (13)
Sanders Draper School

What's It Like To Be Abused?

What's it like when your mum beats you to a pulp?
What's it like when you sit on the stairs and sulk?
What's it like when you've been burnt by your mum?
How would you feel, if your dad called you scum?

What's it like when your body is badly bruised?
What's it like when you've been abused?
What's it like when you're fed once a day?
How would you feel, if you lived this way?

What's it like when you're never home alone?
What's it like when you always have broken bones?
What's it like when you never have a life?
How would you feel, if your mum nearly stabbed you with a knife?

What's it like when you don't sleep in a proper bed?
What's it like with cuts and bruises all over your head?
What's it like when you're the one getting treated bad?
How would you feel, never being happy, always sad?

Kirsty Walker (13)
Sanders Draper School

What Is It Like To Be?

What is it like to be in a wheelchair?
Knowing everyone around you cares,
When you're in hospital, people bring you bears,
But it doesn't heal up the long term tears,
People look down on you,
It feels threatening too,
But you don't understand, I'm just like you,
There is an upside to all the attention,
Because I get a raise on my pension,
I want to get up and walk,
But it is all talk,
Being normal is a dream,
I would love to be part of a team.

Samantha Holt (13)
Sanders Draper School

What's It Like?

What is it like to be abused?
Not knowing what happens next.
Hiding in the pain and shame,
Cut and bruised on the inside and out,
Starved from food, comfort and love.
Thrown around like a ball, from wall to wall.
Try to hide the scars from the outside world,
But wanting to tell of the nightmare
That goes on behind closed doors,
Trying to live a normal life,
But that's not possible when you're beaten and abused.
Having chipped teeth where they were smashed against the wall.
Hoping the neighbours will hear your screams.
Hoping that one day you will be free.

Jade Woodhead (13)
Sanders Draper School

I Wonder What It Is Like To Be . . .

I wonder what it is like to be
A bee flying around with glee
Eating honey?

I wonder what it is like to be a fish
Swimming around
In the deep blue sea?

I wonder what it is like to be a bird
Flying nice and low
Above the clear blue sea?

I wonder what it is like to be a horse
To be able to run around
In a massive field?

I wonder what it is like to be a cat
To run around catching bats?

Alexandria Mason (12)
Sanders Draper School

What Is It Like To Be . . .

W hat is it like to be a child in the war
H appiness would never come to mind
A t the moment my parents cannot be found
T he bombs go off

I 'm on my own
S cared to death

I 'm in my house, it has no roof, I'm in what was my bedroom
T he school was meant to be open, but my family and I
                              didn't get there quick enough

L uckily I'm still here, but they got gassed by a bomb, too much
I want to cry
K illing myself might be an option
E veryone outside might even die.

What's it like to be . . .

What's it like to be beaten by your dad, day and night,
If he didn't want me, he doesn't have to give me a fright,
My head being crushed against the wall, time and time again,
Cuts and bruises over my face and body,
Trying not to think about the pain,
A new black eye every day,
I wish he would just stay away,
Mum won't do anything,
She does nothing,
So help me please,
I'm down on my knees.

Jade Allen (13)
Sanders Draper School

What's It Like To Be Trapped?

People driving
People walking
People shopping
People talking
A normal day began
A day to end in tears.

> Men intent on destruction
> Destroying our most prized construction
> It all happened in an instant
> The end for some, now not so distant.

People screaming in every room
As all of them approach their doom
The fear in their eyes
As clear as night skies.

> You can hear the increasing heart rate
> Was this to be their chosen fate?
> If only you saw this dreadful sight
> The pain their families went through that night.

Being caged with no way out
Is certain death without a doubt
I know this story is not fair
But the man who did it, just didn't care.

People praying
People crying
People screaming
People dying.

> Two concrete trees scraping the heavens
> We will always remember September eleven.

David Walton (13)
Sanders Draper School

What's It Like To Be An Orphan?

What's it like to be an orphan?
To be given away; only two years old
No one there to have and hold.

What's it like to be an orphan?
Not knowing who your mum and dad really are,
But seeing them drive away in a car.

What's it like to be an orphan?
To make new friends to pass the time
But saying they can't come back to mine.

What's it like to be an orphan?
Even though it smells of grime
This orphanage will do just fine.

What's it like to be an orphan?
To want to search long and far
To find the same people, in the same car.

Rebecca Cutbush (13)
Sanders Draper School

I Wonder What It Is Like To Be?

I wonder what it is like to be
A fish in a pond
Swimming in the lovely clear water?

I wonder what it is like to be
An elephant, big and strong
Big, heavy and long?

I wonder what it is like to be
A lion sleeping in the grass all day
Killing animals and going out to play?

I wonder what it is like to be
A hamster, small and short?
I am very short, but I have a lot of thoughts.

Tom Buckley (12)
Sanders Draper School

What's It Like To Be Adopted?

What's it like to be adopted?
Not always knowing who your mum and dad are,
Wondering how long you'd be apart,
Thinking, would they return from afar?

What's it like to be adopted?
Having to settle into a new life,
Would they ever treat me right,
Or would the family and I always fight?

What's it like to be adopted?
To be loved and cherished,
Beginning to feel this hugging and kissing
Is not for real
Hoping this great love won't banish.

What's it like to be adopted?
You may feel very sad,
But also loving all the care,
To tell the truth,
Being adopted is not at all bad!

Jasminder Blah (13)
Sanders Draper School

What I Want To . . .

I wonder what it would be like as a dog,
Seeing through all the fog?

I wonder what it would be like as a queen,
So I could be seen?

I wonder what it would be like as a fish,
But not on a dish?

I wonder what it would be like as a ball,
Being kicked all over the hall?

I wonder what it would be like as a shark?
But wish I could bark.

Callum Oakley (12)
Sanders Draper School

I Wonder What It Is Like To Be . . .

I wonder what it is like to be a fish,
Swimming in the sea, up, down,
Round and round, morning till eve.

I wonder what it is like to be a bird,
Flying through the sky,
Watching the clouds go by.

I wonder what it is like to be a cat,
Just sitting on the mat,
Oh, I wonder, I wonder.

I wonder what it is like to be a banana,
Hanging on the tree,
While I'm singing with glee.

I wonder what it is like to be an orange,
Sitting in the bowl,
All left alone.

Rochelle Green (13)
Sanders Draper School

What Is It Like To Be A Beggar?

What is it like to be a beggar?
Living on the street.
Hear the echo of all the feet,
Not a glance, not a stare,
No one has a penny to spare.

What is it like to be a beggar?
The pain you're feeling is so mega,
Some people just don't understand,
All you want is to be found.

What is it like to be a beggar?
No one there for you to love,
All you wish is to have a home,
What is it like to be a beggar?

Georgia Day (13)
Sanders Draper School

What Is It Like To Be A Child In The Beslan Siege?

What is it like to be a child in the Beslan Siege?
To wake up in the morning and be fine,
Then to go to school and see a scene of a crime.
To be held hostage by strangers,
Being told you were going to die.

What is it like to be a child in the Beslan Siege?
Friends and teachers being hurt
And you're sitting there in the dirt.

What is it like to be a child in the Beslan Siege?
Some of you clothed
And some of you not.
Scared and shaken and out of sight.

What is it like to be a child in the Beslan Siege?
To sit in your class,
Not knowing if you would get out alive or not!

Kirsty Foxcroft (13)
Sanders Draper School

What Is It Like To Live On The Streets?

What is it like to live on the streets?
No food, no water, no home,
It feels so alone.
I can't sleep, instead I just weep,
Days go on and on, it makes me think,
Is there anything to live for?
I wish I was with a family in a home,
At least that way, I wouldn't feel so alone.
Sitting on the floor,
Wondering if I could do much more.
People hurt me by making fun of me,
No one is going to be with me when I die,
I am going to die alone.

Ameer Nasir (13)
Sanders Draper School

I Wonder What It's Like To Be . . .

I wonder what it's like to be,
A bird flying so high?
Wind beneath my wings
And soaring through the sky.

I wonder what it's like to be,
Someone famous, all the glitter and glee?
With all the money,
Nearly everything is free.

I wonder what it's like to be,
On the new Virgin Airline, in space and free?
For four minutes of freedom,
From the gravity.

I wonder what it's like to be,
A photo so still for evermore,
Just sitting in a frame all day?
Wishing I could be more.

Katy Stallan (13)
Sanders Draper School

A Jaguar

What is it like to be a jaguar?
Running as fast as a car.

What is it like to be a jaguar?
Living in the wild.

What is it like to be a jaguar?
Catching animals to live.

What is it like to be a jaguar?
Being seen by people.

What is it like to be a jaguar?
In a zoo all day, in a small cage.

What is it like to be a jaguar?
Lonely and bored and sad.

Perry Smith (13)
Sanders Draper School

I Wonder What It Is Like To Be . . .

I wonder what it is like to be a dog,
Sitting around, being lazy and only seeing black?

I wonder what it is like to be a fish,
Swimming in the sea, having all that space,
Seeing all those bubbles?

I wonder what it is like to be a boy,
Moaning, not doing anything?

I wonder what it is like to be a banana,
Growing on a tree, then being sold in the shops,
Then getting eaten?

I wonder what it is like to be a slug,
Slithering around on the went, cold floor,
When it is raining?

I wonder what it is like to be a bird,
Flying in the sky and going wherever you want?

I wonder what it is like to be a teacher,
Having to put up with all those children
Being lippy, rude and loud?

Chloe Cook (13)
Sanders Draper School

I Wonder What It Is Like To Be . . .

I wonder what it is like to be
A Ferrari 350 with Michael Schumacher
Sitting inside me?
I wonder what it is like to be
A snake rattling in a tree?
I wonder what it is like to be
A horse galloping around with glee?
I wonder what it is like to be
A bird flying from tree to tree?
I wonder what it is like to be
A fish swimming in the sea?

Jonathan Child (12)
Sanders Draper School

I Wonder What It's Like To Be . . .

I wonder what it's like to be a parrot,
Talking all through the day,
Chatting here, chatting there,
In every, single way?

I wonder what it's like to be a boy,
Moaning and groaning,
Eyeing up all the girls,
Saying, 'Nice booty, give us a whirl!'?

I wonder what it's like to be a bird,
Flying up in the sky,
Flapping my wings?
Oh my, oh my.

I wonder what it's like to be a baby,
Crying through the day?
I'd love to be a baby,
Because I'd get my own way.

I wonder what it's like to be a butterfly,
Fluttering my wings
Away from a little caterpillar,
To be beautiful for just one day?

Emily Jeffs (13)
Sanders Draper School

I Wonder

I wonder what it would be like
To be a fox,
Running in the forest,
Getting shot?

They hunt me down, they hunt,
All I can do is duck and dive,
I wonder why?
I wonder why?

I wonder what it would be like
To be a bird,
Flying in the sky,
Nice and high?

I wonder what it would be like
To be a monkey jumping around,
Swinging and clinging to the trees,
As I land on my knees.

I wonder what it would be like
To be a whale?
Wow! That really is a whale!

Terry Bickley (13)
Sanders Draper School

What Is It Like To Be?

What is it like to be,
A child in Iraq,
Where people bomb the parks?

What is it like to be,
A child on the streets,
To never have any sweets?

What is it like,
To be a child who can't read or write,
Who is always getting into fights?

What is it like to be,
A child in Iraq,
Where every day you're crying in the dark?

What is it like to be,
A child with no food,
Where everyone goes, *'Boo!'*?

What is it like to be,
A child with no love,
As your mum and dad are sent up above?

Evelyn Garnett (13)
Sanders Draper School

I Wonder

I wonder what it would be like
To be a dog sitting under a tree?

I wonder what it would be like
If I were a car going around in the road?

I wonder what it would be like
To be a computer doing all that stuff?

I wonder what it would be like
To be a fish swimming around in the sea?

I wonder what it would be like
To be a cat on the street on my own?

Stephen Kiy (12)
Sanders Draper School

Homelessness

What is it like to live on the street?
Scavenging for food, for something to eat,
Looking for places to sleep,
Somewhere dry and something to keep,
No one will give him a job,
To make some money, he has to rob,
He has no friends or mates,
He eats off Tesco value food, like dates.

What is it like to live on the street?
Scavenging for food, for something to eat,
No one there to look out for him,
He spends most of his day, looking through the bin.

What is it like to live on the street?
Scavenging for food, for something to eat,
He has no money,
He tries to nick it off a granny,
He tries his best to beg for money,
But people just find this funny.

Sam O'Vens (13)
Sanders Draper School

New School

The bell has gone,
I'm already late,
New teacher waiting,
Ready to debate.
Class mates stare,
I'm full of fear,
Miss shouting,
I cannot hear.
Second lesson's over,
Four more to go,
Almost home time,
How many days to go?

Grace Brown (12)
Sanders Draper School

Homelessness

What is it like to live in a box?
What happens when it rains?
How do you know what time to wake up?
How do you get comfortable?

Who else would live in a box?
Would it be warm inside?
Where will I get food from?
How long would I go for without eating?

Where will I get my clothes from?
Where will I get money?
Would I watch television?
Would there be a big gang of us searching for food?

Will it be me on my own, waiting for company?
Would I ever hear the radio again?
Would I know what was happening in the world?
Are we at war?

What will I have for dinner tonight?
Will I have something from the bins?
Would it become so extreme, I had to eat bugs?
What is it like to live in a box?

Anneka Louise Fisher (13)
Sanders Draper School

What Is It Like To Be A Child In Iraq?

What is it like to be a child in Iraq?
To fear each and every day,
For the terrifying bomb sounds,
That makes the air turn grey.

What is it like to be a child in Iraq?
Who is lost and all alone,
Who has tragically lost their family
And who sadly doesn't have a home.

What is it like to be a child in Iraq?
Who never sleeps at night,
Praying for hope and peace,
To end the endless fight.

What is it like to be a child in Iraq?
Who always tries to dream,
Of being somewhere else,
Where everything is as it seems.

What is it like to be a child in Iraq?
Who never, ever eats,
Who always loses their appetite,
Because of their lack of sleep.

Sarah Connor (13)
Sanders Draper School

Hostage In Iraq

What is it like to be a hostage in Iraq?
A blindfold over your face, not knowing what's happening.

What is it like to be a hostage in Iraq
With two other people all in the dark?

What is it like to be a hostage in Iraq,
To hear that you will die soon?

What is it like to be a hostage in Iraq,
Pleading for your life? It's no lark.

What is it like to be a hostage in Iraq?
Scared out of your life, of what might happen.

What is it like to be a hostage in Iraq?
Cold, hungry and thirsty, it's no walk in the park.

Kelsey Oates (13)
Sanders Draper School

I Wonder What It Is Like To Be . . .

I wonder what it is like to be a pet fish
Swimming around and around.

I wonder what it is like to be a dog
Loved by its family.

I wonder what it is like to be a car
Driving around the street.
My lady owner keeps me nice,
Clean and neat.

I wonder what it is like to be a bird
Sitting in the tree,
To wake me up in the morning,
Singing just for me.

Emma Hernaman (12)
Sanders Draper School

I Wonder What It Is Like To Be . . .

What is it like to be a child in Russia?
I wonder do they eat at all,
Or whether they always feel so small.
Do they play and do they talk
And in the end, can they walk?
I bet they think about their home,
Wishing they could speak on the phone.
Waiting in silence, waiting to die,
Wanting to get up and spit in their eye.
Sitting, watching people cry,
They threatened us with a gun to our eye.
Finally, the helpers came, I gave a sigh.
Oh my, oh my, I cried, I cried,
Because all I knew, was I survived!

Zoë Lawrence (12)
Sanders Draper School

What Would It Be Like . . .

What would it be like to be impossible?
To fly to the moon and back,
To go through a safari track.

What would it be like to be impossible?
To live for ages, straight,
To beat the rules of fate.

What would it be like to be impossible?
To go down a chocolate mine,
To travel back in time.

What would it be like to be impossible?
Maybe I'll wait and see . . .

Aimee Green (12)
Sanders Draper School

I Wonder What . . .

I wonder what it is like to be a monkey,
That hides in a tree?
After that, it gets to the bottom
And laughs, 'I'm free!'

I wonder what it is like to be a snail,
Slithering slowly
And leaving a trail?

I wonder what it is like to be a chocolate cake,
Put in a cake tin, ready to bake?

I wonder what it is like to be a wave upon the beach,
Pummelling gently
And then leaving to go out of reach?

I wonder what it is like to be a car that goes slow?
It loses every race
And it's just gone, go.

I wonder what it is like
For you to be me?

Craig Harper (13)
Sanders Draper School

What Is It Like To Be Abused?

Some kids are bullied and beaten up
And when they get home, it happens as well,
They are living a life of hell.

Their parents kick them all about,
Now the kids are too scared to scream and shout.

Some are blindfolded and locked away,
Sometimes even for the rest of the day.

When my mates beat me about,
They say they are only playing,
But sometimes I feel like saying:
'How would you like to be a victim of abuse?'

Ashlyn Peek (13)
Sanders Draper School

A Fishy Story

I wonder what it would be like
To be a fish?
Watch them swimming around
And see how they live.
I wonder what bait fish like?
It has to be something
That they can bite.
The only fish with teeth,
Is a pike which bites its food.
I wonder what the fish do under?
Because I know they don't get much space.
So I wonder what it would be like
To be a *fish!*

Danny Woodhouse (12)
Sanders Draper School

Why?

She cries tears of blood and pain,
Not wanting to cut herself again
But the addicted voice inside her brain,
Calls out to her, but she's not insane.

Why? You ask. You question why,
She was once bubbly, but now too shy.
Why does she hide behind her hair,
Hoping people will not stare.

At home she sits up in her room,
A secret stare, knives of doom.
Her new knife, just lightly leans,
Her skin still pierces, she has let off steam.

She is now relieved, the doors still locked shut,
She quickly cleans up the blood from her cut.
At school she's silent as she gazes at the sky,
The children always wonder why?

Joely Smith (13)
Shenfield High School

Death

Silence.
Faint lights ahead.
An odd figure in the night,
Crossing the dark, abandoned street,
He waits.

Claudia Thwaites (12)
Shenfield High School

Ode To Autumn

Season of mists,
And gnarled trees,
Golden leaves,
And no bees.

Mellow fruit fullness all around,
Leaves gliding to the ground,
Harvest time,
Happiness is found.

Rain falls to the floor,
On a bare Sunday morning,
Mum dashes around in her dressing gown,
Only she's up.

Oliver Hazell (13)
Shenfield High School

Autumn Air

The air in autumn feels,
Crisp
Clear,
It soars
Slowly.

Thomas Thackray (13)
Shenfield High School

See The Truth

Self harmer,
Getting calmer,

Drawing pin
Pierced skin,
Can't wait,
Foil plate,
Knowing doubt,
Blood seeps out.

Cloudy mist,
Cut wrist,

Dizzy head,
Bloody red,
Fear's denser,
Tissue dispenser
Windy path,
Blade in bath.

Done bad
Loving sad,

Little kid,
Tin lid,
Aching heart,
Growing apart,
Sharp glass,
Time to pass.

Something said,
Cut head,

Close brush,
Red rush,
Hidden pain,
Going insane,
Dying youth,
See the truth . . .

Laura Juniper (14)
Shenfield High School

Party Night

It was party nite in Landan, and me and my posse
went around town, nickin' some cars and bustin' up enemy gangs.
Dey dobbed on us but we weren't scared
Of da coppers dat came for us.
We bowled it down the road and everyone got out ah way.

We walked into da clubhouse, met up with me homies,
Had a few pints and chilled with me gels
Rappin' to da music, a proper massive crew was in der.
I told 'em dat dis was our turf, so get lost or
We'll have yer. Dey ran off like chickens.

My posse were proper drunk 'cept me, so some went home.
Me and Snapz was hangin' round da town, wen a proper massive crew
Came roun' da corner. Me and Snapz pegged it cos
Dey 'ad baseball bats and pellets on dem. Dey weren't dat fast so
we hid roun' an alley and dey walked past.

We counted ah money 'tween us we 'ad 40 quid of dosh.
We went back to clubhouse and were chattin' to me gels 'bout wat
'ad 'appened.

We was gonna go home but we saw my posse and hanged roun' with
'em in da streets
The proper massive crew turned up again but we had reinforcements
from more mates
Dey weren't scared though, so a proper massive bundle came to us
And we were mullerin' 'em.

We won da fite but all of us was injured with loads of blood, so we
went home
And rested, ready for tomorrow nite, cos we knew wat was comin'.

Stephen Cozens (13)
Shenfield High School

Dancing

She walks on the stage
The spotlight hits her
She dances
Soetes, eschape, pliates
The audience stares
Their eyes watching her every move.

She leaps, turns, spins
They can't believe it,
All eyes on her.

It's all dark, apart from one light,
One light on her
She dances.

It's the final moment
Her last moment
She falls
But curtsies on
And walks off
Their eyes follow her
No applause, no sound
Nothing.

Abigail Potter (12)
Shenfield High School

Hallowe'en

Darkness awakens
Threatening pavement yawns
Shattering lampposts, below stars
Waving, screaming, yawning, crashing
Morning comes.

Chloe Steer (11)
Shenfield High School

Self Harm

People stare and wonder why
I harm myself in such a way

How I can feel the cold surface of a knife,
Against the skin and risk my life.

Why through the anger and the pain
I feel the need to cut again.

Well to feel the knife slice through my skin
Makes me feel OK again.

To see the blood pour makes the anger,
Depression and doubt depart.

But still it leaves me in slight despair
As the sadness begins to restore.

As those 10 seconds of release are needed
More and more.

Hanna Lander (13)
Shenfield High School

Ode To Autumn

Brick walls and
Concrete floors
Cover the wheat and
The fields of rye.

Autumn's odour
Such a bad pong
The birds are singing
But are out of their song.

Skeletons are now about
Scaring the poo out of little Scouts
The Devil has now scarred for life
When the Grim Reaper comes round with his scythe.

Jamie Barnwell (13)
Shenfield High School

Tissues And Scar Tissues

Bloodstained tissues on the bathroom tiles,
Mutant scar tissues cover harmed skin.
They cower under my fake smiles,
Acting like trophies for pain within.

Red tears drip from myself like rubies,
Glimmering in my adrenaline.
Pathetic peers who thought they knew me,
If they did, shrinks would be flooding in.

I hide under my jumper sneering,
Hunched up under my paranoia.
All around me, my world's caving in.
I'm not careless and free like before.

Bloodstained tissues on the bathroom tiles,
Mutant scar tissues cover harmed skin.
They cower under my fake smiles,
Acting like trophies for pain within.

Harriet Austin (13)
Shenfield High School

Beneath Skin Deep

My heart pounds like a drum against my ribcage, rattling my bones.
I dig my sharp teeth into my gum until I taste the sharp, salty blood
                                        trickling onto my tongue.
I clench my fist and press my nails into my sweaty palm until there
                                        are visible dents in my hand.
It's no use.
I run my finger across the cool, steel blade, lift it to come into contact
                                        with my scarred skin and pierce.
A rush fills my body, but this time it is not a rush of relief or satisfaction.
This time it is a rush of pain. Pure pain.
A small river of blood twists and weaves down my arm
A bright yet invisible light has been, suddenly, switched on.
There is no more hiding in the dark . . . there is no more dark to hide
                                        in.

Kaz Melvin (13)
Shenfield High School

Big Blue Eyes

Scrape the flesh and pick the wound,
Blade dampens the happy mood
There was once a man who said all the world's a stage
That man was right, my acting to hide the blade.

Big blue eyes
Hold in the pain
Big blue eyes
Hold in its rain
Big blue eyes
Too frantic to see
Big blue eyes
Frown upon me.

Public too busy, too busy to see
The pain that's afflicted upon me
Scissors and knives and Stanley blade too
Lie around the crimson loo.

Big blue eyes
Hold in the pain
Big blue eyes
Hold in its rain
Big blue eyes
Too frantic to see
Big blue eyes
Frown upon me.

Scrape and cut that's all I can do
Emotion bouncing like a kangaroo
Blood trickling down my arm
But I still remain tranquil and calm.

Big blue eyes
Hold in the pain
Big blue eyes
Hold in its rain
Big blue eyes
Too frantic to see
Big blue eyes
Frown upon me.

April Lipscomb (13)
Shenfield High School

Ode To Autumn

Season of rain
And cold, dark mornings
Where great trees stood, only skeletons remain
Shadows of their former self.
Its life and blood scattered around
By the harsh, unforgiving winds
Frost strangles the remains of life
Mercilessly choking all it touches
Only the big chain stores survive in this barren wasteland
                                    acting as a haven
To the parasites this race has become.
Youths run amok throwing eggs, burning things,
Playing with fireworks
Is this what it's about?
Gorging on sweets and sitting
Not moving from the telly.
Even animals give up
In this lonesome season.
No more they dance, leap, flutter about.
No life,
No more.

Tommy McGroder (13)
Shenfield High School

How Different

They say a problem shared is a problem halved,
When I shared mine they just laughed.
Looking down their noses in disgust,
But it's the only way, you know I must.
It relieves all pain I have bottled up inside,
When you say you'll listen, I run and hide.
I came to you for help once before,
But you shut me out and closed the door.
You don't understand the emotional struggle,
All you had to do was give me a cuddle.
A little laugh and a joke, that's all.
Kisses, compliments, anything at all.
All I needed was love and attention
I needed your help, did I forget to mention?
I hope you're happy now you've left me in this state,
I pick up the bread knife resting on the plate.
My emotional scars can now be seen
Oh how different it could have been.

Sophie Harvey (13)
Shenfield High School

Hallowe'en

Late at night
No cars in sight
People get a fright
The witches and ghosts come out
Nobody dares to come out
Ghouls start to scream and shout
Trick or treaters loom
Waiting in the gloom
The mummy comes out of its tomb
    On Hallowe'en!

Sarah Truesdale (11)
Shenfield High School

Hallowe'en

Hallowe'en is coming
Shut your doors
Hallowe'en is coming
Can you hear the scrape of the claws?

The ghosts are out
They come through your loo
The ghosts are out
Whoooo!

The zombies are back from the dead
Are your hairs tingling on the back of your head?
The zombies are back from the dead
Are they under your bed?

Remember . . .
Hallowe'en is coming
Be afraid
Hallowe'en is coming
Be very afraid!

Frank Austin (12)
Shenfield High School

Tormented

It was just teasing
Words as sharp as blades,
That was it at first,
Then violence took hold,
And my life turned sour.
When I think of them
I mark myself
Feeling only joy,
Joy that suffocates
A blood filled ritual
The screaming crimson
Covers my cold skin.

Kirsty Hough (13)
Shenfield High School

Winter

Winter sweeps in
Trees are bare
Streets have a white coat
Like an old man's hair.

Trees so plain
Brown all over the bark
The chill of ice all over
Cold makes it feel so dark.

And over the night
A white coat there
Trees now better to see
Being so fluffy and fair.

The old man wakes up
Sits in the chair
Looks at the world
Wishing he was out there.

Will Ashby (12)
Shenfield High School

Slash

The blade drifts down on to my soft, silky skin
The blood oozes out, it's about to begin.

The anger and the pain has built up inside,
But I let it all out and watch the knife slowly glide.

As my arm suffocates in red, bubbling foam
I hear the key in the door, my parents are home.

I race up the stairs then hide the knife in my drawer,
When the next time they're gone I'll enjoy it once more.

Charlotte Moody (14)
Shenfield High School

Extinction

It walks like a lion
Runs like a cheetah
Never stops hunting
Feeding on the human kind
It sleeps all day
Kills in the night
Only one can stop them
And they are waiting for a fight
Humans are in the middle
Their war has just begun
No one can hear them
Death has just begun
No army can take control of this war
The extinction of human kind is on the line.

Keshav Patel (12)
Shenfield High School

Hallowe'en

The darkness of the night,
The costumes that give you a fright.
The howl of the wind,
The lights that have been dimmed.

The cackle of people,
The ring of the bell on the church steeple.
The chewy, gummy sweets,
The voices of children shouting trick or treat.

The sound of eerie music,
The people inside are dancing to it.
The silence after midnight,
Everyone is going to bed to sleep tight.

Alistair Bygrave (12)
Shenfield High School

The Child

The falling body lands,
On the concrete that lays beneath it,
The crackling bones
That follow.

The once-loud boy is quiet
No laughter from him now
Dismantled like a broken toy
His bloodied face covered.

No hope for this little boy
No chance for him to stay
The endless slumber he must sleep
For this little boy

The child no more.

Rebecca Morement (12)
Shenfield High School

Bonfire

Bonfire
Reaching up with fiery fingers,
Cackling and crackling.

Bonfire
Roaring and burning the wood underneath
Scorching my back, pushing away the darkness.

Bonfire
Scaring away the cold
Licking trees and bushes nearby.

Bonfire
Eating away the black night
Flicking and swishing in the wind, but the light will not go out.

Lydia Mihailovic (11)
Shenfield High School

The Evil Ones

When even the wolves lie low
And the crowing ravens won't crow
Dragons whimper with fright
Where wolves hunt throughout midnight

Prey screaming with fear and pain
The evil ones fear no shame
Battling through the rain
Nearby prey in sight.

As they creep stealthily through the abyss
Growing hunger causing a hiss
They sneak up and *strike!* But they miss . . .

With the first ray of the morning light,
They slink back towards their lair
Thinking of their only care
It's the end of Hallowe'en night.

Rebecca Hunt (11)
Shenfield High School

Hallowe'en

H orrible noises in the night
A llows the children to scream in fright
L ots of candy shared in trick or treat
L ittle children hate it, but they have to face it
O nly the bravest of people get out of bed
W hen all of this night, fills them with dread
E ating candy is the best part
E ven when it becomes too, too dark
N obody will stop the children from playing their part.

Roberta Leary (11)
Shenfield High School

Sunshine Up High

S hining up high
U p in the sky
N ear the settling moon
S tanding like she owns the sky
H iding behind the fluffy clouds
I n the game of her life
N ear the distance of the stars
E dging their way past.

U ndepending on the moon
P opping its way past the sun.

H iding the sun behind the black blanket of life
I n the sky
G oing to go back down under
H aving the time of her life.

Katie Webber (11)
Shenfield High School

Fireworks Night!

F ire, fire, flaming lights
I n the dark sky they explode so bright!
R adical sounds, crackling noises
E verywhere is beautiful
W onderful, sparkling colours
O oze and whoosh through the sky!
R ipping the clouds' floating coats,
K eeping quiet, trying not to be loud
S eeking the beauty of the sound.

N othing can be seen apart from a shining beam
I n and out the rockets fly
G reatly zooming by
H igh, high, high in the sky
T onight the fireworks fly!

Libby Clark (11)
Shenfield High School

Colours Of The Rainbow

C olours can show how you're feeling
O ver the moon, or under the ground
L ovely colours get shown off
O thers you don't see at all
U nited together they make our world
R ed, yellow, pink, green, orange, purple, blue
S o everyone have fun.

Becky Green (11)
Shenfield High School

Hallowe'en

H orrific sights of ghosts and ghouls
A nd the lights go out
L ittle girls and boys on their own
L ittle ghosts appear
O pen up your fears and frights
W ith all your might just scream
E choing through the hollow house
E nd comes and the night is over
N ow just wait for next year!

Leanne Bolger (12)
Shenfield High School

Hallowe'en

H allowe'en is scary when I trick or treat
A witch goes flying through the sky
L oud and lurking, the ghosts float by
L icking the dead cats, the demon dogs lie
O oo whoo
W acky all night
E veryone is horrid
E veryone is bright
N ice and spooky on a Hallowe'en night!

Jayla Hands (11)
Shenfield High School

Hallowe'en Screams

H aunted houses creek in the darkness
A ll the ghosts laugh out loud
L ittle girls screech and scream
L arge pumpkins on the window alight
O wls hoot and scare the people
W illow trees brush in the wind
E veryone turns into zombies
E veryone dies with a loud scream
N ever ever trick or treat.

Janay Lee (11)
Shenfield High School

Autumn

The leaves on the ground
Brown,
Broken,
They crush
Crunch.

Jonathan Burns (13)
Shenfield High School

Hallowe'en

H allowe'en, are you scared of the dark?
A nd ghosts, plus ghouls
L iquorice, lemon bonbons and sweets you never heard of
L ots of toilet paper and eggs as well
O ne piece of candy for you, one for me too.
W hining children with tummy aches who've eaten too many sweets
E veryone who goes out never comes back the same
E very person who gets candy, gobbles it in their mouth
N o one is left hungry until the next dying day.

Sarah Dare (11)
Shenfield High School

Hallowe'en

Hallowe'en is great
It's great because the sweets
I gobble them all.

Sweets are very good treats
Sweets vanish straight away, yum!
There is one problem.

Big boys steal your sweets
That's why they are gone so quick
Soon *they* will be sick!

Megan Field (11)
Shenfield High School

Autumn

The leaves on the grass
Brown,
Bronzed.
They lay,
Lifelessly.

Alex Dean (13)
Shenfield High School

The Inner Pain

The pain I cry,
Is the pain inside,
The scarring left, is all I see,
Nobody knows what it's like for me,
I think someday, near in the future, I'll be sussed
Somebody, anybody, will discover my cuts,
Round and round the same old routes
I'm sick of my guilt and I'm sick of my wounds.

Natalie Smith (14)
Shenfield High School

Ode To Autumn

Time of colour
Time of bliss
Time of spirits
And real long lists

Shops are opened
Shops are full
Shops are empty
And over priced markets call.

Colour here
Colour there
Colour swarming
As leaves tear.

Fireworks sparkle
Fireworks glow bright
Fireworks soar
Out into the night

Time ticks
Time tocks
Time flies by
As the season clocks.

Conor Robinson (13)
Shenfield High School

Hallowe'en

H allowe'en what a fright
A mazing costumes I see through the night
L ots of scary features come at the door
L oads of bags full up with sweets
O h my, chocolate galore
W ow, my bag is over flowing
E at them up in
E very way
N ow I'm full up, I'm gonna be sick!

Tierney Kelman (11)
Shenfield High School

Fireworks Night

F ighting bangs waiting to be freed
I s that the Catherine wheel spinning round and round?
R umbling noises increasing in the sky,
E erie squeaks sparkling bright.

W hirling stars fly everywhere
O nly see them when it is dark,
R ound the sky the fireworks go,
K ids are holding sparklers in their hands,
S taring at the fireworks until they *stop!*

Zoe Amenumey (11)
Shenfield High School

Autumn

The leaf on the tree stirs
Rustles
Restless
It writhes
Wriggles.

Scott Fenn (13)
Shenfield High School

Hallowe'en

H allowe'en is fun
A nd scary
L ots of sweets involved
L ots of screams from everywhere
O f horror from people's souls
W eeping children from the dark
E ating what they find
E veryone that joins in
N ever is themselves again.

Sarah Kay (12)
Shenfield High School

A Scary Night

H allowe'en, a scary night
A ll are out and ready to fright
L ots of costumes
L ots of sweets
O h, I think I have eaten too many sweets
W hen you go out to trick or treat, beware!
E erie, spooky, creepy, is there somebody behind you?
E veryone wary of what's about
N ever leave home without your eggs and toilet paper.

Nicole Webster (11)
Shenfield High School

Autumn

Leaves on the air float
Flying
Freely
It crunches
Crumbles.

Ryan Spurge (13)
Shenfield High School

Tactics

The ball came out of the hard hitting scrum
The scrum passes to the fly half
The fly half gets it down the line
Fly half gets it to the winger
Winger gets hit hard by prop
Winger offloads it to inside centre
Centre passes to fullback
Fullback runs for it
Tttrrryyy!

Guy Prince (13)
Shenfield High School

Never Noticed Nobody

I welcome death, but it's never here
Instead it's brothers pain and fear.

I fear the pain, the pain is fear
And a vicious circle does appear.

A small cut, over time
Grows into a wound, I've committed a crime.

Psychiatrist can predict it,
But once turns into twice and soon you're addicted.

Life and death don't seem to matter
Blades and flesh, from your mind, just won't scatter.

I tease and taunt the veins in my wrists
The blade digs deep, you get the gist.

Reality becomes pretend
Pain becomes my only friend.

People frown and wonder why
But keep it hidden and they'll pass by.

My life is one of dark corners and long sleeves
As easy to see as a summer breeze.

I hide away, I creep, I lie
And no one will notice me till the day I die.

Jenni Stewart (13)
Shenfield High School

Autumn Leaves

The leaves off the trees
Float,
Fall,
They glide,
Gently.

James Davenport (13)
Shenfield High School

All Hallows Eve

Hallows eve, the clock strikes twelve, midnight.
Bloodstained ghouls, gory, dismembered, midnight
Eerie, disillusioned, unearthly, weird, midnight
Phantoms and poltergeist, witches cackling, children
screaming, midnight.

Blood-curdling, intimidating, shivers down your spine, midnight
Panic, the end is nigh, you can't turn back, midnight
Souls breathing, grieving, haunting, midnight.

Lurking, chilling, watch out, they're coming for you, midnight
They're out to get you, they grab, hands like rock, weighs
on you, midnight.
Shadows, darkness, chilling, watch out they're out to get you,
Out to get you,
Out to get you,
Midnight.

Emma Clayton (13)
Shenfield High School

All Hallows Eve

All Hallows eve
Hear the witches breathe
Feel the chilling air
When the spirits are near.

The cackles of the witches
Give me the twitches
The swooshes of the witches
Going through and under ditches

Watch out
Don't turn your back!
On All Hallows eve

Charlotte Chambers (13)
Shenfield High School

Red Hot

Red hot burning bubbles burn inside me,
Unseen pain pierces my inside body.
Red hot burning strokes slice my outer shell,
The pain unseen suddenly becomes real.
Red hot tears trickle gracefully down my pale skin.
My body pays the price of scars
Stop it girl! Stop it!
But I can't! I can't, I can't,
If I stop slicing, I'll end up vomiting *red hot* liquid.
Why do I harm?
I harm to stop suicide
I harm because no one *loves* me
No one will ever *love* me
I can't stop ever, no way
I can't stop not until my unseen, unreal *red hot*, burning
Surging pain has been *cut . . . cut* away from me.

Phoebe Barns (14)
Shenfield High School

Hallow's Eve

Witches fly on Hallow's eve
You may not see them, but you better believe.

A black cat sitting on the drive,
Don't run him over or you will not survive!

Witches sitting around a cauldron making spells,
Beware of the terrible smell.

An old woman with a pointed hat,
Swoops down on a broomstick and grabs the cat.

Is it imagination, or is real?
I'll stay indoors in case they kill.

Emma Knight (13)
Shenfield High School

You Don't Understand

You don't understand me
You don't understand it
You don't feel the yearning
I always get.

You see the sharp blade
But don't feel the need
You don't sense the sharp want
I always receive.

I am now safe
I know I'll be calm
Smooth, sharp and savage
It cries for my arm.

I close my eyes tight
And my pain is released
I am now flying
I have found relief.

Your hands demand how
Your face questions why
Your eyes seem to wonder
Why it's red tears that I cry.

You don't understand me
You won't understand it,
You'll never feel the yearning
I always get.

Nicola Murray (13)
Shenfield High School

Autumn

The red leaves falling look,
Scarlet,
Crimson,
They rustle,
Scuttle.

James Loveard (13)
Shenfield High School

My Secret Shame

One scarlet burning stroke
It permeates my entire body
Like one continuous electric shock
The crimson bandage starts to soak
Like a mother it will comfort me
Like medicine it will heal
My inner fears, from all the years
Are now written in black and blue
Tears of blood spill from my veins
I bleed out all the bad inside
But the scar that will mark my skin
Will be impossible to hide
It bears the burden of my pain
Along with sympathy
It was just an accident, I shall claim
And live with my secret shame.

Sarah Taverner (14)
Shenfield High School

I Feel The Need To!

Here I am all alone, yet again no one here.
It's in my hand, this sharp blade, I can see my face shimmering
My sleeve rolled up, my wrist is clear, I'm ready now, ready.
The door is locked and no one can hear
Suddenly, *stomp, stamp, stomp.* It's my mum!
'Dear, are you OK?'
'Fine, Mum, honestly, just washing my hands, be down soon!'
As she leaves I can't do it, I don't feel the need
'Why not?' I ask myself
My body has taken control at last and I can go another day
Without feeling that need.

Christina Smith (14)
Shenfield High School

All Hallows Eve

On a wintry, cold and gloomy night
It was All Hallows eve
Don't come out, you'll have a fright
Strange happenings, things you won't believe.

As the old church clock strikes twelve
There is movement all around
The clock stops chiming
And the zombies come out of the ground.

The old grey headstones fall to the side
As the ghouls begin to rise
It's been a whole year since they last came out
But it makes no change to their size.

The dark sky is suddenly transformed
As the souls and spirits meet
The ghosts arrive and it's party time
Better known as trick or treat.

The friendly ghostly spirits
Have great fun in their time
Slowly moving gravestones
In the mud and slime.

As the sun begins to rise
You need have no more fear
As all is quiet again
And will be for another year.

Sophie Roberts (13)
Shenfield High School

Autumn

The leaves falling sound
Crispy,
Crunchy,
They fall,
Flutter.

David Mais (13)
Shenfield High School

Self Harm

S tinging is what they feel inside
E verlasting pain
L ove is what they're deprived
F orever with them - pain

H atred is what they feel,
A gony is what they hate
R emember; look, the scars tell the story
M ates are what they need, *mates.*

Michelle Pateman (14)
Shenfield High School

My Friend

S tained red towels that were once white
E ffect is instant, blood over my eyes
L ife seems better now, seeing better light
F eels happier, relieved and calm.

H elp from a friend, essential for my head
A nger when my friend won't cut
R anging from my school to my bed
M y trail of blood behind me.

Jenna Sargeant (13)
Shenfield High School

Get Help

S lit your wrists and make it bleed
E verything's better now
L eave it for a while then do it again
F ree from the pain inside.

H arm is not good, please stop
A sk for help and sort it out
R eal love for you is not lost
M any people want to help.

Laura Butcher (13)
Shenfield High School

Relief

Relief is sweet if you did not know
True feelings hidden, only the scars show
Flesh feel fresh as it drips away
It's an instant relief from a stressful day
It's like adrenalin pumping through your veins
Grabbing that glass from the smashed windowpane
To help this stop, all you have to do
Is tell the distressed one,
I am here for you.

Hannah Page (13)
Shenfield High School

Worries

I hate my life, I hate myself
I have many worries
Nobody likes me, I am lonely
I have many worries
The pain inside cannot be seen, I am forever faking
I have many worries
I am an actor, hiding bloody tears
I have many worries.

Then with one single slit all of my worries flood out
In the thick red blood
Now I have no worries . . .
But for how long?

Sarah Wright (13)
Shenfield High School

The Dark Is . . .

The dark is like an ashy friend with gleaming eyes,
The dark is an owl with eyes as big as a button.
The dark is shadows creeping behind every object
The dark is nothing to be afraid of don't worry it won't bite.

Abigail Hill (12)
The King John School

10 Reasons To Get Out Of Bed

My sleeping eyes close even tighter still
As the sun escapes and reflects upon my window sill.

It rudely awakes me, but should I complain?
The day looks inviting, to miss it would be a shame.

As my senses awaken
I can smell eggs and bacon.

I could lay there for the next hour
But what about a nice shower?

I can hear the TV
But what can it be?

Should I let my curiosity get the better of me?

I didn't pack my bag last night
I can see it on the floor, what an ugly sight

The post has just come through the door
It could be the CD I've been waiting for

I really do need to get up
I would just hate to be late.

I'm dying for a cup of tea
I hope there's enough milk left for me.

I've just found the perfect excuse to get up
It's *Saturday*, hooray for that day.

Ryan Birnie (13)
The King John School

War

War is a rattling train
Like a broken down roller coaster
Sounds of bombs exploding
A dark, gloomy night
Tastes like red-hot steel
Feels like freezing cold ice cubes.

Lucy Bloxham (11)
The King John School

The King John School

I am a student of King John
I have been for a term
I love the school
It's where I can learn

Footy, rugby and running
I love to do the lot
The girls say I'm stunning
What a load of old grot

I have some great mates
We get on well
I have no dates
I think that's swell

My teachers are fine
They teach me well
I'm always on time
I think that's swell

I'm going to sign off
Nothing else to say
If that's O.K
I did it my way.

George Bradley (11)
The King John School

Anger

Anger is a speeding bullet
Like a crying wolf
Thunder crashing
Snow white
Taste like burning ice
Feels like death
So anger is cruel.

Emma Lee (11)
The King John School

Bullying

As I make my way to school each day
And see the children skip and play
I will ask the bullies in my school
'Can you be kind and not so cruel?'

But as I enter I can hear them say,
'Here comes fatty, you can't play,'
And it starts from there and lasts all day
I cannot stand it, go away!

Because those who bully don't understand
It can send a child to the Promised Land
It happened to me when I was seven
But now I'm safe and up in Heaven.

No bullies here to make me cry
Because God protects me, not let me die
Unlike the teachers I have known
Who left me scared and all alone.

To those who drove
Me to my grave
You're just nasty bullies
So be ashamed.

Peter Gardiner (13)
The King John School

Anger

Anger is a baby crying all night,
Like a *devil* in the night,
Foxes crying in the night,
The colour of devils
The taste of sick bubbling in your throat
Feels like a cup of coffee spilt
All over you.

Matt Redmill (11)
The King John School

What Would I Do Without My Dogs?

Who would be there on a cold winter's morning
So warm, yet so calming?
What would I do without my dogs?

Who could I take for a walk in the cold autumn breeze
As we struggle through the wind?
What would I do without my dogs?

Who would greet me with a lick and excitement
In the hot summer's day?
What would I do without my dogs?

Who would be there in the spring buds
To roll across the cool, cold grass?
What would I do without my dogs?

Who would be there in the lovely lust cold frost
To keep me warm and feeling loved?
What would I do without my dogs?

Jay Clark (11)
The King John School

Love Is . . .

Love is like a daffodil gently flowing in the breeze of summer
It sounds like a heart beating softly
Love is multicoloured, because love has good times and bad times
Tastes like a candlelit dinner
It feels like soft new bedding on your bed.

Love is a feeling you get deep down inside
It sounds like a flute playing a smooth duet
It is magnolia-white, calm and gentle
Love tastes like fresh chocolate cake just been baked
Feels like a continuous buzz coming from a bee.

That's what love is . . .

Jessica Robinson (11)
The King John School

The Tiger Cub And The Monkey

There once was a tiger cub and a monkey
The monkey was quite funky!
The tiger was bright and full of strong might.

They lived in the jungle
In a huge great bundle
The house was full of leaves and twigs
But smelled strongly of old greasy wigs.

'Let's decorate this dump!' said Tiger
'I agree,' replied Monkey with a bit of a jump.

By the end of the week
The house was all sleek
In gold and white sheets
It smelled very sweet
Of honeysuckle and rose petals!

Gabrielle Wright (11)
The King John School

Sea

The sea is green
It's not very clean
The sea makes you go crinkly and look very old
Oh! Did I mention you come out cold
The sea is full of fish
Some like to catch them and make a dish.

The sea is green
It's not very clean
The sea is rough out in the middle
And I am not very good at making a riddle
Pirates used to own the sea
But now it has been set free.

Anthony Kell (14)
The King John School

My Cat Died

My cat died
And I cried
I took him to the vet
They put down my pet
The next day
I did say
They put down my pet.

James Gray
The King John School

Anger!

Anger is a ferocious beast
Like a roaring tiger
Waves crushing
Ruby red like blood
Tastes like a spicy, hot curry
Feels like an erupting volcano
It smells like smoke, from a bright burning fire
It twists your mind, and winds you up
Things said in rage, that comes to boiling point
And that sounds like anger.

Amit Lal (11)
The King John School

Anger

Anger is a big black hole
Thumping hard against your head
Axes chopping
Rough veins
Yellow crisp teeth
A teardrop from a weeping eye.

Jody Lapslie (11)
The King John School

The Vampire

Eerie, ghostly and full of bats
On the door peg, a bowler hat
I've a feeling someone's here
A mysterious presence is lurking near.

As I carry on to the living room
There's a creak in the floorboard, under lays a tomb
I sat down to turn the TV on
Then there's the ghost opera, singing their song!

As quick as lightening, upstairs I shot
Then I see his teeth rot!
His bony fingers are a skinny snake
And for the vampire's weapon, a rusty rake.

The vampire is a scream for help,
I ran to save being squeezed to a pulp!
Out of the house, I sprint for bed
'It was only a dream,' Mum said.

Paul Capon (11)
The King John School

Why To Get Up In The Morning

If you're thinking about something bad that happened yesterday
Remember life can turn 180 degrees, in a matter of ways
Today you may come to a crossroad, with 4 different paths to choose
Some you'll win, some you'll lose.

For now you should cease the day
Life's not predictable, you're the artist and life's like your clay
Staying in bed is taking the easy way out
Make the most of everyday fear and not have a doubt

For you might meet Prince Charming today
And you don't want to throw that chance away
So get out of bed
And come what may.

Leah Skelton (13)
The King John School

Midnight Owl

The moon suffocated the sky with its ebony black cloak
Nothing dared move
As the clock struck midnight with one final stroke
The trees brandished bare branches menacingly
Two amber eyes pierced the darkness
Deep from within a dark, decrepit tree
With one shrill cry that punctured silence
The creature protruded from its secret annexe
Swooping smoothly as though in defiance
The crisp white so opposing the black sky
Like a plastic bag billowing in the wind
One short, sharp twist, clear what is was about to try
Shot like a bullet from a gun
It pelted petrifyingly towards the earth
Pulling out suddenly as though scorched by the sun
Squirming silently in its beak was the helpless prey
As the sun rose then glared at it from behind a cloud
Swooping softly, silently, returning, as night made way for day.

Kate Eldred (13)
The King John School

Football

Commotion in the tunnel, waiting to come out
The whistle blows, twenty-two men begin
The crowd cheer as loud as a hundred foghorns blasting in the misty
morning air.
Here comes the ball, right to me, will I pass or shoot?
Time running out, I spin and begin to run
It feels like chains are weighing me down
Just the keeper to beat.
I kick it
It soars as hard as a cannonball, but it's in
Yes we win!

Jonathan Willson (13)
The King John School

Going To War . . .

I am on this small, lonely boat,
But yet I am not alone,
As I have hundreds of eager soldiers willing
To give their life for their country.
The boat pulls up on the sandy coasts of northern France
I had to keep low,
Trying to cover myself under the blanket of darkness.
I dodged the spotlights that were as bright as the morning sun.
On the signal I was told to attack
I sat there waiting patiently for the signal,
I was nervous but yet determined.
My mouth was as dry as a desert,
My heart was pounding furiously
Like a steady beat of a drum
I found myself gasping for breath
Then I heard the signal
'Go, go, go!'
My heart was beating faster than ever, but
I knew what I had to do.

Lana Smith (13)
The King John School

Seasons

In autumn when the leaves turn red
And then they all drop dead

Leading into winter, when the world turns white
And there's dark, dark nights

Along comes spring and melts down all the snow
There are sweet-scented smells and lots of things to grow

Turning into summer, when we're all on fire
The sparkling seas are what I really do admire

I wish I knew how the seasons change
It takes just a year and then it starts again

Lydia Bradford (11)
The King John School

Peace Not War

At the end of this tunnel there is a new light
It's warmly inviting and coming in sight
But war is stopping us reaching the end
It's taking us time so messages we send
Fighting each day, will it ever stop?
No, there is too much suffering so obviously not
Each day innocent children cry with fear
Is the end for us coming near?
War is a fight for everybody's rights
Explosions go off and make bright lights
All that is won is pointless, prevailing pain
All of the families have nothing to gain
For there is an end to all this strife
Yes there is a way to begin a new life
If we all work together to achieve our goal
None of us will ever have a guilty soul
Peace is out there where everyone loves
And messages from God are sent by white doves
This place smells of cotton candy, fluffy and sweet
And the sounds of birds are like a lullaby, what a treat
We can feel the gentle air upon our face
We knew these days would come so let's not brace
Peace is tranquil, like a still millpond
And now everybody uses free time to chat and bond
For now we are in this all together
And that's how it will last forever and ever
That is our dream of hope and we search
Behind every door and creature that does lurch
For peace is our destiny we shall reach it soon
But until then they fight by the light of the moon.

Holly Scally (13)
The King John School

When I Was . . .

When I was one
I sucked my thumb
When I was two
I loved the zoo

When I was three
I learnt how to wee
When I was four
I fell flat on the floor

When I was five
I learnt how to jive
When I was six
I got some drumsticks

When I was seven
I was in chocolate heaven
At the age of eight
Nine's next, I really can't wait

When I was nine
I learnt what was mine
When I was ten
My friend was called Ben

When I was eleven
I discovered 007
At twelve years old
I started to grow bold
Now I'm thirteen
I don't like my room clean.

James Geary (13)
The King John School

Where Is God?

I lay on my back looking up at the sky,
Watching the clouds glide gently by.
Are you there, God?

I'm on a boat out at sea
I look down at the water beneath me.
Are you there, God?

I'm on a mountain, looking around
It's very quiet, there's not a sound.
Are you there, God?

I'm in a cave, everything is black,
I call out but my call comes back
Are you there, God?

I'm on holiday in Devon
I think to myself, is there Heaven?
Are you there, God?

I lay on my back looking up at the sky
What will happen the day I die?
Are you there, God?

Mitchel Davison (12)
The King John School

Fear

Fear is my best friend stealing my boyfriend
Just like a child crying in Africa
Black as the cats on the streets
The sound of an ambulance
The smell of a dead relationship
A premature baby
My Granddad dying
My brother going to war

Madilaine Rowley (11)
The King John School

Anger

Anger is a howling wolf,
Like a caged up animal,
Winds banging, waves crashing,
Everything's vein red,
It tastes like back washing vomit,
It feels like you've been lunged by a knife.

Jon Lofthouse (11)
The King John School

Love

Love is anything you've ever wished for
Like a pair of doves flying through the clear sky
Sounds like church bells chiming
The white of a wedding dress
Tastes like the smooth smell of cream
Feels like the smoothness of a cat's fur.

Leanne Saunders (11)
The King John School

Love

I love your glistening eyes,
Sparkling in the sun,
Your lips are like ice,
Gleaming in the moonlight,
When I am with you I am touched by angels,
You blow my troubles far away,
I feel life is worth living,
I feel complete when I am with you,
Like a bunch of dazzling roses,
As delicate as your skin,
So love is worth knowing.

Darryl Emerson (11)
The King John School

My Favourite Teacher, Mrs Monk

My favourite teacher is Mrs Monk
She is so funky
She probably gets home and jumps about like a monkey
She is the best and wears a big dress
She has a big draw full of sweets and more
Liquorice, toffees and cream

My favourite teacher is Mrs Monk
If you enter her room you'll be rid of your gloom
For here's some advice, she's terribly nice
But beware of the mice up her sleeve . . .
If you ever meet her, her feet do stink
Watch out, she has goldfish in her sink!

My favourite teacher is Mrs Monk
If you make her red, then you are so, so *dead*
If you flick a clip, then she'll do a flip
And there'll be a thousand lines for you!

Emily Pacey (11)
The King John School

My Puppy

My puppy, my puppy
Just doesn't know what to do
She wants to play
She wants to lay
She wants food
She wants to run
What do I do?
I say, what do you want to do?
And she looks at me
I want to do everything
She's a good dog
Like a teddy bear
Taste like sweets
Feels like wool
But she's just a bit busy.

Hayley Newbury (11)
The King John School

My Poem

The sun is shining
Making everybody happy
The sun is shining
Having lots of fun
It's raining
Everybody's complaining
It's raining
We're all stuck inside
It's snowing
We're all having fun
It's snowing
We're all freezing cold
There's a tornado
Picking everyone up
There's a tornado
Sucking every building up
There's a flood
Drowning everybody
There's a flood
Sinking all the houses.

Claire Thomson (12)
The King John School

Anger

Anger is a big fire
Just like a burning building
Tango orange
A clicking clock
Burning ash
Hot lava
The burning sun
A flaming torch.

Stefan Turner Powell (12)
The King John School

Anger

Anger is a tiger
Pouncing on its prey
Blood-red
Burning forest
Raging sirens
Bitter lemon
Wounds inside that don't show
Tears that won't go away
My anger is.

Abigail Harman (11)
The King John School

My English Teacher

My English teacher is the best
She is better than all the rest
She gives us things like loads of tests
And she always expects us to do our best
She comes from a land far away
That we call the USA
She jokes and laughs and makes us giggle
And that is why she is the best teacher of all

Ben Henderson (12)
The King John School

Anger

Anger, a fiery blade
Like a grizzly bear
Screaming
Like a scab red
Feels of red-hot fire
Tastes of poison.

Joseph Williams (11)
The King John School

Happiness

Happiness is a world full of joy.
Like everyone surrounding you is cheerful and kind,
Friendly faces everywhere.
The skies are blue, the sun is shining bright,
Just right for outdoor stuff.

Happiness is when you have something to do:
A hobby or sports or something meaningful in life -
Caring and sharing and contributing.

Happiness is when you have someone that loves and cares for you
Being with good friends and my family.
Imagine you're laying in the streets all cold and
No one to care and love you.

Happiness is when you have something to look forward to.
There are very rich and very wealthy people that just
Buy and buy, but then they have nothing to look
Forward to and live an unhappy life.

Etienne Fourie (12)
The King John School

10 Reasons Why I Get Out Of Bed

I get out of bed to smell the bacon
I get out of bed, wake up my brother
I get out of bed to look at my hair
I get out of bed to see my cat
I get out of bed to smell the fresh air
I get out of bed to pester my mum
I get out of bed to watch cartoons
I get out of bed to have my horrible breakfast
I get out of bed to try and be glad
And I get of bed to go to *school*
That's ten reasons why I get out of bed.

Leah Nichols (12)
The King John School

My Brother

When he wants a favour
He's as smooth as a salesman
Pointing out benefits
Of his generous terms
But when he doesn't get his way
He's a lion denied its prey
Growling and grumbling
And pacing up and down
Or a car engine without petrol
Coughing and spluttering
And refusing to budge.

Give him pen and paper
And he'll scribble strange shapes:
Double-jointed monsters
Self-destructing laser guns
Lean-to houses with smoky chimney stacks
And a bloated blueberry boy
That is meant to be his older brother -
Me!
. . . So last night
I put him in a guillotine and cut off his head,
Which promptly said,
'I'll tell on you for being so mean!'
It was only a dream,
After all!
But someone please tell me what I can do
With a boy as impossible
As my brother Stu!

Aryan Mardanpour (12)
The King John School

Love

Love is sharing time with each other
Love is helping someone in need
Love is friendship with friends and relations
Love is a happy family
Love is a brother and sister playing together
Love is a group of happy people
Love is a newborn baby
Love is people having fun
Love is caring for each other
Love is the whole world coming together as one
Love is the way you show your feelings for people
Love is a feeling floating in the air
Love can grow with time
Love is all around you
Love is hugging and kissing
Love can affect the way you live
Love is not a threat
Love is how you act with people
Love is giving
Love is not someone who hates
Love is everywhere you go
Love is how you treat animals and the wildlife
Love is how you react to things
Love is deep in your heart
Love will never go away
Love will never die or fade
Love is a happy feeling
Love is a bath of melted chocolate
Love is the heart of everything.

Sarah Jane Fuller (11)
The King John School

Love And Hate

Love is like an orchid about to bloom
Like the sunshine in the morning
As pink as candyfloss
A heart beating
Freshly baked bread
A warm mug of cocoa
A cosy pair of slippers
A bouquet of carnations

Hatred is a volcano waiting to erupt
Like a bomb plummeting to the ground
Black as a stranger's shadow in the night
Cats fighting
Petrol burning
A black hole swirling
A dog's face bleeding
Jumping in front of a train
Dead.

Kelly Hodges (13)
The King John School

Betrayal

Betrayal is like a dark sea on a furious stormy night
Once betrayed I'll never trust again
Friends tossed aside like an old sock
Confidence gone, doubt will consume me
Like an incurable virus, the end is inevitable

Family to the rescue, no ego here
Assuring words like snowdrops begin
Summer rays dawn new growth
Self assured new friends I'll make
A mighty oak I have become.

Gregory Vail (12)
The King John School

Hate

Hate is a gun
Just like a ferocious bull
Timber wood brown
Huffs and puffs
Dead person
A bike out of control
Broken bones.

Michael Bellenie (12)
The King John School

Anger

Anger is like a book with pages
Like a pack of wolves
Trumpets blowing in your head
Black paint
Tastes like Brussels sprouts
Feels like sandpaper.

Henry Howard (11)
The King John School

Anger Poem

Anger is like a destructive devil
Like a vicious tiger
Like a screaming baby
Witchy-black
Like you've swallowed a plank of wood
It feels like you've been slowly picked apart!

Zoe Harvey (11)
The King John School

A Chimpanzee's Story

I live each and every day with fear
These two-legged creatures coming nearer
Its twig swaying by its thigh
Ready to strike
This power hungry beast
No mercy to be concealed in it
Its red-tinted eye staring at me
It strolls over to my sanctuary
My sanctuary has been lost to the beast
Still he strolls
Petrified I am still
The creature enters mine
It takes a step in
I back away from pressure
I scream and shout for help
This only aggravates
It raises the twig
With an ear-splitting crack is brought back down
A pain seizes through me
A wicked smile of success
It has finished
My sanctuary returns for a few more hours
It's petrifying presence withdraws from my cage
The petrifying presence
Of man.

Rebecca Horgan (11)
The King John School

Love

Love is a big red heart
Spring flowers just begun
Birds whistling, leaves falling
Romantic midnight sunset
Icing on a wedding cake
Stars shining in the midnight sky.

Bethan Macey (12)
The King John School

Untidy Kylie

There was a girl called Kylie
Who never kept things tidy,
Her room was a mess,
But she couldn't care less,
And she wasn't very smiley.

You could never get out or in,
She said she'll tidy up in a min,
But of course she never did,
Because all her stuff she hid.

She was playing with matches one night,
And she set her bed alight,
She couldn't get out the door,
Because stuff was all over the floor.

Kylie survived a very near death
But in her room there was nothing left.

Safely use matches to set things alight
Or like Kylie
You might see a white light.

Chloé Norton (11)
The King John School

Anger

Anger is a fire,
Hot like a coal poker.
Blazing orange,
Burning smoke.
Fire crackling,
Tasting like warm water.
Crying inside,
But brave outside.
Maybe tomorrow it will be okay.

Sophie Mansfield (12)
The King John School

My Morning Routine

First I wake up to the tongue-piercing ring of the alarm
Before lying there, enjoying the relaxing feel of my warm bed
After I make my bed, I finally can see as soon as I step into the light
And I realise what the night has done to my face and hair, as it had
almost looked alright the night before.

I then feel refreshed and awake as I slosh the cold water on my face
Before covering up my naked and natural skin with the usual
                                                    clothing for school,
While I listen to the usual music, I hear creaks along the floorboards as
my siblings start to wake up
Then realising what a state I'd left my room in, I fix it up, bringing
                                                              light in.

I come down the creaky stairs and see the grin on my mum's face as
she bids me good morning,
While I listen to the lecture my stomach is giving me,
Searching the cupboard I find my usual cereal
As I pour it out, the loud clatter of them echo through the house.

As I munch on my cereal I wake up my dad, who then chucks a wind-
up to me about something else embarrassing,
Which I try to ignore and enjoy the fresh taste of my breakfast
Until I feel that cold, tingly feeling and when I look down I notice the
milk stain on my shirt
And my mum's grin turns to a frown as she wipes it off leaving a much
bigger mark.

From then I carry round with me the rank smell of milk
Which eventually I forget about
And focus on my hair or looks at the last minute
And when I go out finally, it still looks a mess.

Amy-Laura Austin (13)
The King John School

The Mysterious Light

I was standing on a hill up high,
When a flickering light caught my eye.
It was very bright and all ablaze,
It seemed to be in the middle of a maze.
I felt the need to explore,
And found myself at the maze's door.
I walked through the magical archway of leaves,
And found myself in a maze of trees.
The maze, of course, was very tricky,
It also hurt as it was very prickly.
Round and round, here and there,
I searched for the light everywhere.
Suddenly, around the bend,
I found myself at the journey's end.
There it was, a wooden torch,
Burning brightly with flames that scorch.
Its flame was orange, red and gold,
But strangely the air was very cold.
I stared at it for hours and hours,
It seemed to have magical powers.
It pulled me closer to its heat,
But I felt the need to retreat.
I turned around and ran in fear,
I didn't stop until the hill was near.
Safe on the hill, I turned to gaze,
One last time at the torch in the maze.

Ben Moxom (13)
The King John School

Hate

Hate is like a tornado whirling around
Just like a burglar robbing your house
Black-eye black
Knock out punch
The atmosphere around you
Blood shot eyes.

Joe Hitchcock (12)
The King John School

Daffodils

Moving softly in the night
And by day consuming light
Nice and slowly they come to bloom
To take away that lonely gloom
Beautiful colours, orange, yellow and white
To make our moods more happy and bright
With the wind they slowly dance
Lovely movements send us in a trance.

Sophie Howard (11)
The King John School

Anger

Anger is a destructive devil,
Like a vicious tiger,
Like a screaming baby,
Witch-black,
Like you have just eaten a plank of wood,
Feels like you have slowly been picked apart.

Daniel Whybro (11)
The King John School

Fear

Fear is like a cat and mouse
Just like a wrecking ball at 100mph
Icy white
Screaming dog
Melted cheese
Monster
Trembling child
Tidal wave ready to hit.

Ben Strohmer
The King John School

School

School can be cool if you rule
So beware of the teacher that wears no underwear
Teachers pick on the ones that take the mick
The thing about teachers is that they have smelly feet
So do not meet the feet
Teachers can be fun, school can be fun, so anything can be fun.

Chay Silver (11)
The King John School

Love

Love is a special place, always in our hearts,
Although it might be painful,
It sometimes keeps us apart.

Love is like a rose, loving as can be,
Red like a cherry,
Graceful like instruments playing softly.

Love is like chocolates,
Bursting with sweetness.

Claire Whitworth (11)
The King John School

The Grizzly Bear

My favourite animal is a grizzly bear,
It's known to be scary and wild,
But it has beautiful brown hair,
Other times they can be tamed and mild,
Their favourite food is fish.

That the bears catch from the river,
But they don't eat it out of a dish,
People say they live in the forest
And people say they live in caves
But they can get stuck in the waves.

If I had my own grizzly bear I would call it Norris,
But if it was a girl I would call it Doris,
I would let it live in my garden,
As it will be too big for the house,
Unlike my sister's mouse.

Charlotte Scannell (11)
The King John School

Love Is!

Love is butterflies that dance
By our tender skin,
Touching our tingling hands.

Cupid's arrow that found you both
Love is cherubs formed in a heart
Smothered in kisses and warm cuddles.

Cherubs that walk beside you
Leaving a trail of goodness and
Treasured love.

The smiles on their silk faces are filled
With light and joy that hug you in a silk coat
Leaving us with a warm feeling inside.

Bethanie Cousins (12)
The King John School

Hell And Heaven

Hell is a red ball of fire
Just like a destructive bomb destroying the world
Flamed red
People dying
Scorched flesh
Burnt slaves working
Skulls being crushed
A killer werewolf.

Heaven is a bunch of roses blooming
Just like a baby being born
Milk-white
Angels dancing
The smell of perfume
Angels flying around
Eternal life
Heaven's gates opening
People being saved.

Louis O'Connor (13)
The King John School

Anger

Anger is like a burning fire
Hot like the glowing sun
The colour of bloodshot red
The smell of black smoke
Anger sounds like an angry thunder storm
The taste of gone off milk
Anger has eyes that are really scary
Anger is rain that never ends
Anger is something you can't control
Anger is a fierce dragon
Anger is the sound of children's pain.

Lucy Hollister (11)
The King John School

My Hamster!

Truffles is my hamster,
Truffles is the best,
Truffles is my hamster,
She doesn't like to rest.

Her fur feels like silk,
She really loves her milk.
Truffles is really fun,
She has her very own run.

She loves to run on her wheel
She likes her very yummy meal.
She likes her warm and cosy bed,
She always wants to be fed.

I'm her best friend,
Her tubes like to bend
Truffles is a prankster,
Truffles is my hamster.

Alice Hendry (11)
The King John School

Anger

Anger is a dog chasing a car
Rising like a rocket going up to space
Fire burning red
Fresh horse manure
Police pounding down the road
Chicken gone-off for a month
Red eyes burning in the wind
Tears constantly falling on a soft pillow.

David Havill (11)
The King John School

Love Is . . . !

Love is the leaves rustling to the beat of the whistling wind
The silent rain off the rooftops smashing on the ground
The cold ice drops trickling down my throat
The silky sun rising up to the sky
Breezy wind throwing itself towards me.

Anna Elizabeth Roberts (11)
The King John School

Fear

Fear is *red*
Like a raging bull in a stadium
It sounds like screaming children in the night
It tastes like blood when you bite your tongue
It feels like being alone in darkness
It reminds me of death.

William Campbell (13)
The King John School

Starting A New School

Starting a new school is usually very cool
It's generally lots of fun; you don't want your mum
The food is really nice, they even serve rice
The sports are really good, do them - you should
Most of the teachers are great, none of them I hate
Secondary school is best, although homework makes you stressed!

Patrick Neary (11)
The King John School

Anger And Love

Anger
Anger is a howl in the woods
Like a screaming baby
Cymbals clashing
A pitch black cat
Tastes like a rotten bone
Like a sharp needle.

Love
Love is romantically sweet
Like a smooth heart
Laughter crashing
Violets swaying
Tastes like a bottle of champagne
Like a heavenly breeze.

Luke Snoad (11)
The King John School

The Stormy Sea

The stormy sea is lining up in the dinner hall
A tsunami is a dragon's rage
The sea is a monster lying asleep till it is time

The sea breaks all asunder
Cracking bones like thunder
Lying awake hearing it roar
The wall bursts
Death comes on swift wings for those who meddle in her business.

James Lovell (11)
The King John School

Hate

Hate is a snake looking you in the eye,
Just like death in your worst nightmare,
Blackness hovering
Fireworks cracking,
And the fear of death still quacking,
In the thin air on Earth.

Jealousy is your mate winning a game of football
Like the stench of breakfast, your mum is eating
Fire burning
A ship turning
And a rich boy making fun of you.
You feel like dying
So you do so.

Steven Ashwell (12)
The King John School

The Sea

The sea is calm as a pancake
The sea is a bowl of blueberry juice
The sea is wavy as hair
The sea is blue as a dolphin
The sea is rough as wood
The sea is a shimmering cloth
The sea is a water fight
The sea is blue as printer ink
The sea is a big bath with blue bubble bath
The sea is blue as the sky
The sea is a big blue piece of paper
The sea is topsy-turvy as an aeroplane
The sea is windy as a fan.

Lizzie Esdaile (11)
The King John School

Rainbow

The rainbow is a colour spell
To give the world its colour,
The rainbow comes when all is dull
And sets our hearts a flutter.

A sunbeam streaks across the sky
To light up all the grey,
We make a wish the rain will go,
And come back another day.

A crock of gold is what we seek
At the rainbow's end,
To make all our dreams come true
And our troubles to mend.

Red, yellow, pink, green
Orange, purple and blue,
Are some of the colours that we've seen to make
Our dreams come true.

A leprechaun as we've been told
Stands guard over our pot of gold,
Those who disbelieve this story
Will never find this golden money.

A rainbow is a colour spell
That sets the sky alight
I hope I find that pot of gold
To make my heart take flight.

Sophie Stennett (12)
The King John School